girls
just
wanna
have
impact
funds

This book is about making the world a better place by aligning your investments with your values. Therefore, we dedicate it to Marianne and Shailendra, the first people who invested in Female Invest, enabling us to build a company that has changed the lives of women across 100+ countries. As our earliest supporters, they invested much more than money; they invested their time and unwavering support.
We wouldn't be here without it.

girls just wanna have *impact* funds

A feminist guide to changing the world with your money

From the founders of *Female Invest*

Contents

Money can change lives.

Money provides the power to live life on your own terms; the power to be independent; and the power to support causes that you care about. When we talk about money, we often talk about how it impacts us as individuals, shaping our personal opportunities in life. But we rarely discuss how money can be used to change the lives of others—not simply through donations, but through investments.

Making money while making a difference is a powerful concept that has the potential to change the future, because every time we spend money, we cast a vote for the future that we want to live in—for ourselves and generations to come. It's time for women and marginalized voices to own their financial power and unleash their potential as changemakers in a world that so desperately needs it.

What to expect from this book

This book is not an introduction to investing—we already wrote that, it's called *Girls Just Wanna Have Funds—a Feminist Guide to Investing*. Instead, this book is the ultimate guide to making money while also making the world a better place. We want to mobilize the financial power of private investors to solve some of the world's most pressing issues. We especially want to mobilize the financial power of women, because they have, historically, been systematically excluded from positions of power—and this continues today.

Humanity is now facing existential threats, and women are not always being included in the conversation about how to solve the problems that arise at the top of governments or companies. Therefore, although this book is written with women and nonbinary people in mind, we invite anyone who wants to change the world for the better to read it and learn from it.

Why impact investing?

Around the world, women are much more likely to donate their money than men.[1,2] At the same time, women are more likely to volunteer for social causes and donate their time, too.[3] This is great, but there is one problem: you can only spend your time and money once. The good news? By spending just a little time researching investment opportunities that benefit others, you can use your money to create positive change for others while growing your funds at the same time. This way, you'll have even more money (and power) to contribute to change and to create a positive impact on the world.

WOMEN: A FORCE OF POWER AND CHANGE

Around the world, the focus on impact investing—using your money (and thereby power) to create a positive impact on the world—is skyrocketing, and women appear to be a driving force behind this change. Of course, this shouldn't come as a surprise, because women have long been known to make financial decisions based on what's best for their children and their wider family. However, now women are also increasingly taking a bigger-picture view. They are aligning investments with what they feel is best for their community, their neighbors, and the planet.

Global wealth demographics have their part to play in this trend, too. Women, overall, have more money than ever before, which makes us a sizable economic force that controls a third of the world's wealth. In addition, women are increasing their wealth faster now, adding $5 trillion to the wealth pool globally every year and outpacing the growth of the wealth market overall.[4]

Clearly, given their growing financial power, the values that women hold will shape how wealth is created, mobilized, and passed down to the next generation. This is important, because women are more efficient in acting on issues such as climate change and social injustice,[5] and countries and companies with more women at the top generally have more ambitious climate and social policies.[6] At the same time, research shows that women make great investors.[7] So imagine how much change could happen if we unlock the potential of women.

IS THE CLIMATE CRISIS *MAN* MADE?

This question is provocative—we get it. But hopefully what you're about to read will provoke you even more. Let's start with the facts: we are facing an existential crisis in the most literal sense of the word, because the world as we know it "is in a state of climate emergency," according to the UN.[8] The climate crisis is not a new phenomenon, and scientists have been warning us about this for decades. In 2019, 11,000 scientists signed an open letter stating that

the climate crisis is "threatening natural ecosystems and the fate of humanity."[9] With such an existential threat at our doorstep, now seems like a good time to act. However, despite increased focus on this important topic, organizing a sufficient international response and slowing the rise in global temperature has yet to happen. The international efforts to solve the climate crisis seem to have been characterized by one thing: lack of female involvement.

At COP27 (the UN's annual climate change conference) in 2022, only seven out of the 110 government representatives attending were female. This seems ironic, as research consistently shows that women care more about sustainability than men and are more likely to be change-makers for climate change.[10] Joycelyn Longdon, Founder of Climate in Colour, explains: "When more women are elected into parliament, stronger environmental bills are passed and they're enforced more strongly, more strictly."[11] As a result, countries with more female politicians and leaders have better climate policies and lower recorded emissions. In addition, female investors are almost twice as

As of 1 January 2023, only 7.6% of world leaders are women.

likely as their male counterparts to validate the importance of integrating environmental and social factors into investment policies and decision-making.[12] With climate a key concern for populations around the world, you'd think women would be elected like never before, but as of January 1, 2023, only 7.6% of world leaders are women.[13]

We know women are severely under-represented in government, but the same is true among the big companies that are playing an increasingly important role in tackling climate change. That's not just through responsible production, but by championing the invention of new products. However, female representation is not looking great here, either. Among the 500 largest listed companies in the US, only 8% have female CEOs.[14] Among the 350 largest listed companies in the UK, that number is only 4%.

Women are included less in discussions on climate change but are impacted more by the consequences. Aside from being excluded from decision-making, women also suffer disproportionate impacts of climate change. Not only

Research shows women are more likely to take action on climate change and social injustice.

do they suffer greater economic repercussions, they also bear an additional burden of unpaid care and domestic work, have less access to resources, and are pushed to drop out of school or marry early to manage the family's financial stress.[15] According to the United Nations Development Program (UNDP),[16] 80% of people displaced by climate crises are women.[17]

Knowing this, could the climate crisis have been avoided, or at least minimized, if women had been involved in the decisions that have been made which have impacted our planet? We will never know.

It's often said that money can't buy happiness. We disagree.

MONEY
ISN'T FAIR

It's often said that money can't buy happiness. We disagree; money can buy you food, shelter, security, education, and access to healthcare. However, access to making and managing money isn't fair. In fact, it's totally unfair.

It would be easy to make a case of men versus women, but the reality is much more complex. Looking at it on an international level, the poorest 50% of the global population share just 8.5% of total income.[18] At the same time, the richest 10% earn over 50% of total income. The difference becomes even greater when looking at total wealth instead of just income; this is because the wealthiest 10% of people in the world own 76% of total wealth.[19] In the future, these inequalities will grow as the impacts of climate change are felt more acutely in lower-income countries—among those who did the least to cause it, of course.[20]

However, financial inequality does not just exist *between* countries, it also exists *within* them. The level of inequality within any given country or community depends on many factors, including gender, race, sexuality, and class. These inequalities may overlap, and they extend across generations. As a result, the cycle of inequality is difficult to break because some people are disadvantaged from the outset. In this way, the access to making and managing money is totally unfair both between and within countries. For example, women of color experience discrimination differently from white women in a society that affords privilege to whiteness. Disabled people face barriers that can mean they aren't able to participate in work to the same extent as non-disabled people; trans women don't have the privileges of cisgender women, and migrants are often excluded from the very financial systems that we want to help you understand.

The wealthiest 10% of people in the world own 76% of total wealth.

IT STARTS WITH RESPONSIBILITY

Every decision made that involves money has an impact on the world around us—from the smaller ones about what to eat and where to shop, to the bigger ones about where to invest. Interest in socially responsible investing has increased at a different pace around the world; in the US, it took off during the Covid-19 pandemic, where ESG funds captured $51 billion of net new money from investors in 2020—a record, and more than double the net inflows in 2019, according to Morningstar research.[21] ESG stands for Environmental, Social, and Governance, which refers to a set of criteria used to evaluate a company's sustainability and ethical impact. We'll get back to this in more detail later (see page 27).

However, making conscious choices with your money is not as simple as it may seem. We want to make this easier, which is why we've written this book. We'll focus on how you can make an impact through your investments, and we'll break down some methods of investing sustainably and putting your money where it will make the world a better place. This idea of combining investment power with the desire to have a positive impact is often called impact investing. Throughout this book we will cover the ins and outs of what this impact investing entails, as well as the many moral dilemmas it gives rise to.

The history of money

The concept of money was invented before the beginning of written history.[22] In ancient times, this was primarily in the shape of commodities being traded for something else. This early trading quickly became tricky to calculate and very difficult to scale over larger populations and big land masses. This is where the idea of money as we know it came in. In the seventh century BCE, the first standardized coins were created in what is now western Turkey[23] (other sources claim it happened in China)[24]. Fast-forward to the modern day, money is the foundation of society and there are over 180 currencies circulating in the world.[25]

The UN estimates it will take 140 years to achieve equal representation.

Women hold significant financial power— and it's time to use it.

It's time to act

At the current pace of progress, climate change will have permanently transformed the world before women get equal representation—which the UN estimates it will take 140 years for women to achieve. In addition, scientists warn that we have eight years to avoid a climate catastrophe.[26] We can't wait any longer; it's time to use the hard power that we do have—financial power—and we need to do it *now*.

Women are becoming educated at record rates and are accumulating wealth like never before, and we also direct the vast majority of consumption—in fact, in the US, it's estimated that women make 80% of all purchases.[27] While this may be rooted in outdated gender roles of women shopping for the household, that doesn't change the power dynamic. Knowing this, what would the world look like if we started setting demands such as only shopping from companies that demonstrate responsible production and diverse leadership? Only supporting politicians who align with our values? Women may be excluded at the top of governments and companies, but we can force these same institutions to follow our values if we collectively start setting demands with our money.

It's time to take matters into our own hands by utilizing the power we have at our disposal: money. This book is not just about how to make impact investments and feel good about ourselves, it's about stepping into our financial power and using our money as our voices to change the world.

What is impact investing?

Impact investing: doing well by doing good

Most people need a sense of purpose in their life in order to feel happy and fulfilled. But while the desire to make a positive difference is as old as humankind, the best ways to do it have dramatically changed in recent years.

Traditionally, the act of financially helping others and supporting causes you care about has been associated with giving away money. But what if we told you that it's possible to make your money grow in the process, too? This is where impact investing comes in.

Impact investing vs sustainable investing

There are no official definitions of sustainable/impact investing, and different scholars all have different opinions on the technicalities. In this book, we'll use the following definitions:

Impact investments: Investments made with the intention to generate positive, measurable, social, and environmental impact alongside a financial return.[1]

Sustainable investments: The practice of analyzing a company's environmental, social, and governance (ESG) risks and their opportunities.[2] In this way, sustainable investing and impact investing are two related but different approaches. As described by Dr. Hakan Lucius, Head of Corporate Sustainability at the European Investment Bank: "The key difference between sustainable investing and impact investing is that sustainable investing tends to be more focused on ESG integration and risk management, while impact investing is focused on generating positive impact and creating change."[3]

WORRIES AND REFLECTIONS

Writing this book has come with several worries and reflections, because impact investing has sparked controversy around the world. As the topic is a relatively new one, there are no official definitions of this term, which is why different studies with different focus areas and timelines have varying answers to how impact investing performs compared to the overall market. Despite the conflicting results, one thing is certain: only investing in impact investments makes it hard to diversify your portfolio, which increases risk and reduces the likelihood of achieving the average market return. What does this all mean? It means that no matter what approach we take in this book, we'll face criticism from scholars who are using different definitions.

But we've decided to write this book anyway, and we've put in countless hours of research to make sure these chapters offer investors a well-rounded, easily understandable introduction to the topic.

Impact investing is a meaningful way for investors to put their money where their values lead.

Myths about
impact investing

Before we dive into the specifics of impact investing, first let's debunk the myths.

1 **An investment either makes an impact or it doesn't**
We're sorry to break this to you, but there's no such thing as a perfect investment. When it comes to personal values, different investors have different views and priorities. Looking for the perfect investment is almost like looking for love; even though you have a wish list, you'll have to compromise on some areas. And just like the desired traits of a romantic partner are defined differently by different people, your values when investing are unique to you. Whether you want to focus on diversity, the environment, or something else, only you can make that decision.

2 **Impact investments give a lower return**
This question has been debated endlessly, because there's no clear answer to it. The graph on the next page shows the performance of a group of impact investments versus a group of traditional investments. When comparing the two lines, there's no clear winner; some years the sustainable investments did better, but in 2022 traditional investments did better largely due to the war in Ukraine and the major increase in price of oil and gas products (industries that are typically excluded from most impact funds).

There are many impact funds available, and their impact/profit can be measured in different ways. Many claim to have proven that impact investments are actually better, while others claim the exact opposite. Depending on the source, time period, and investments used in research, both sides can probably be right in different cases. Overall, we feel confident in saying the results are generally mixed—and there is a good reason for that.

Returns of sustainable funds vs. other funds in the U.S 2019-2021[4]

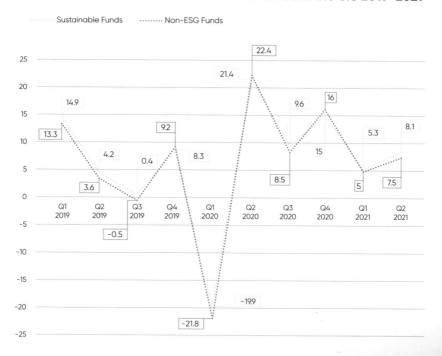

········· Sustainable Funds   ········· Non-ESG Funds

Let's have a look at 2022—a very turbulent year for the economy, to say the least. In 2022, oil companies outperformed many sustainable investments. Why? Many oil and gas companies profited from the war in Ukraine, which led to rising oil and gas prices in Europe and across the world. In other years, such as 2020, strong-growing tech companies that are often heavily contained in sustainable indexes, due to their low carbon dioxide output, outperformed the market as a whole and therefore also caused sustainable index funds to perform well.

How many of these results can be attributed to the fact that these companies are considered impact or not, and how much impact simply came down to the line of business in which they operate and external circumstances, is often hard to say.

On average, the returns of a sustainable or impact portfolio are similar, if not better, than portfolios without an impact or sustainable focus. So, why not invest with impact, if it doesn't make a difference to your returns?

 It's difficult to invest with impact
Impact investing doesn't have to be difficult; it's all about having the right tools and knowledge, and once you've read this book, you'll be ready to start the journey.

Frameworks for *evaluating impact*

There is no official definition of impact investing, and the topic can be frustratingly fluffy, but there are a number of widely acknowledged frameworks that can be used to evaluate your investment. In the following sections, we'll go through these one by one.

Disclaimer: Before diving into the frameworks of impact investing, we need to add a warning. This is because even though the impact of what you're about to learn is exciting, these frameworks can be painfully boring and dry. This is probably part of the reason why they aren't common knowledge, so we'll do our very best to guide you through.

Did you know?

A study by RBC Wealth Management found that women are more than twice as likely as men to say it's extremely important that the companies they invest in incorporate ESG factors into their policies and procedures.[5] The shift in financial power suggests women are well-positioned to drive growth in ESG and effect meaningful societal change with their investment dollars.

ESG

To determine whether an investment has a positive impact, the ESG (Environmental, Social, and Governance) framework is used by both companies and governments alike. This framework is helpful for evaluating and categorizing companies based on how they contribute positively to society. So, what does this mean?

E stands for Environmental.
Is a company polluting the air, sea, and land? Or are they participating in renewable energy schemes? Think all things planet-friendly.

S stands for Social.
This is looking at the impact a company has on its stakeholders, such as suppliers and the local communities. This also includes important aspects of the company's workforce, such as diversity and human rights issues for employees.

G stands for Governance.
Assessing how the company is run, how decisions are being made, and how the needs of external stakeholders, such as investors and governments, are being met. Some people argue that governance is the most important aspect, because in the end it's the leadership of a company that decides how that company would act within environmental and social aspects.[6]

ESG investing is intricate due to the absence of a universally agreed-upon standard. Nevertheless, various regions are witnessing the emergence of fresh frameworks and regulations like SFDR and EU Taxonomy (details to follow). Consequently, it's crucial for each investor to personally determine which practices, values, and ESG objectives hold the greatest significance for them.

Where do I find this information?
Most companies do ESG reporting, and this information should be easily accessible on their website, in a separate sustainability report, and/or in their annual report. However, there are also different websites that gather this information. A good one is www.refinitiv.com/en/sustainable-finance/esg-scores. The methodology employed by Refinitiv is particularly appealing, even though they use their own distinctive approach to assigning ESG scores, which introduces a notable element of subjectivity. However, they deserve credit for openly sharing these scores with the public and making their website so user-friendly.

THE SUSTAINABLE DEVELOPMENT GOALS

Have you heard about the UN's 17 Sustainable Development Goals? These are also known as the SDGs and they were agreed in 2015 by all UN members.[7] They focus on topics such as education, poverty, climate change, and peace, and the intention is to include every person on the planet in them.

What's special about the SDGs is that they put a lot of focus on the private business sector rather than only focusing on what governments can do. This makes good sense, given how powerful the private sector is.[8] As the responsibility has become shared, accountability of businesses to be transparent in their action toward achieving the UN's goals is much greater. This means that investors can see more clearly what businesses are doing, how they're trying to improve the world, and how they compare to other similar businesses.

The SDGs include 17 goals, but these are further broken down into 169 targets. To make it easier, these targets are divided into five overarching themes, known as the 5 Ps.[9]

The 5 Ps:

People—Poverty and hunger just aren't acceptable in our modern world, and the UN 2030 goals aim to eradicate these issues entirely.

Planet—The clue is in the title —all things climate change and environment. The situation is urgent and we need to do something.

Prosperity—This progresses from the idea of simply eradicating poverty to striving to ensure that all humans can live comfortable and fulfilling lives.

Peace—World peace is on most of our wish lists, but we're still not there on achieving it. Building societies devoid of fear and violence is another important goal.

Partnership—Last but not least, working together is key for instituting change. Building strong partnerships, regardless of nationality, race, gender, or any other diversifying factor, is essential to making the world a better place and achieving the UN's goals.

2
Planet

CLEAN WATER AND SANITATION   RESPONSIBLE CONSUMPTION

CLIMATE ACTION   LIFE BELOW WATER

LIFE ON LAND

1
People

NO POVERTY   NO HUNGER

GOOD HEALTH   QUALITY EDUCATION

GENDER EQUALITY

3
Prosperity

RENEWABLE ENERGY   GOOD JOBS AND ECONOMIC GROWTH

INNOVATION AND INFRASTRUCTURE   REDUCED INEQUALITIES

SUSTAINABLE CITIES AND COMMUNITIES

5
Partnership

PARTNERSHIPS FOR THE GOALS

4
Peace

PEACE AND JUSTICE

SFDR

SFDR stands for Sustainable Finance Disclosure Regulation. It does sound painfully boring, and it certainly has the potential to be just that, but please keep reading anyway, because it's an important tool for comparing and identifying funds.

The SFDR is made by the European Commission with the purpose of providing better transparency.[10] This means that all investors wanting to put money into a European investment fund now have a set of rules they can use to compare different funds, so they can easily evaluate how sustainable the fund is in order to make an informed decision.

All funds within the EU have to be categorized within three different levels of sustainability, so if you are interested in investing in sustainable funds, looking to Europe is definitely helpful. Most major trading platforms will allow you to buy European funds, even if you're not based in the region. Let's look at these three categories, which are known as "articles."

Article 6
Funds in this category offer the lowest level of sustainability. Article 6 is the default classification of funds, meaning that it may also apply to those funds that have limited or no ESG focus at all.[11]

Article 8
One step up from Article 6 are Article 8 funds. These have set up specific criteria for environmental and social practices within the fund. This means that certain sectors or companies that harm the environment might be excluded, such as oil and gas, tobacco, etc.

Article 9
At the highest level, you have funds categorized as article 9. In these funds, sustainability is integrated as a goal in the investment strategy. The fund is not only screening out certain sectors or companies but choosing to include companies that are the best in their class in terms of sustainability.[12]

Where to find this information?
If a fund has been rated within the SFDR, the article it belongs to will be clearly stated. Some trading platforms have the option of filtering for a specific article, but for those that don't, you'll have to google it.

THE EU TAXONOMY

The EU is really blazing the sustainability trail, and following on from the SFDR regulations, it has further developed the EU Taxonomy. This is designed to make sustainability reporting more transparent for both companies and investors. This classification system currently targets large listed companies, but smaller companies and those with activity in the EU will be included, too.

Companies can classify how much of their financial activity is taxonomy-aligned. This allows for a calculation where you measure the proportion of their overall earnings that align with the taxonomy, essentially assigning a score to the company on a scale from 0 to 100:

- Climate change mitigation.
- Climate change adaptation.

- Sustainable use and protection of water and marine resources.
- Transition to a circular economy.
- Pollution prevention and control.
- Protection and restoration of biodiversity and ecosystems.

In order to align with the taxonomy, companies must live up to all of the following statements:

- Making a substantial contribution to at least one environmental objective.
- Doing no significant harm to any other environmental objective.
- Complying with minimum social safeguards.

This will be used by large companies as well as investment products— such as funds, bonds, and other large financial instruments.[13]

Did you know?

For companies that fall under certain EU directives, it is mandatory to put this information in their annual report so that it is easy to find. This information is very reliable, because as opposed to many other sustainability measures, companies need to have external auditing to confirm the results.[14]

SCOPES 1, 2, AND 3

If you're on the hunt for a quick, all-encompassing overview, you'll find that the relatively straightforward measurements of scopes 1, 2, and 3 are cropping up more frequently when it comes to gauging a company's greenhouse gas emissions. The brains behind this framework? The Greenhouse Gas Protocol.

Scope—This is the most direct measurement, encompassing the greenhouse gases emitted by a company during the direct provision of their products or services. If a company is singing its own praises about its scope 1 achievements, it's a commendable step, but there's more to explore.

Scope 2—The second scope takes into account emissions from purchased energy. This includes emissions from electricity powering factories or offices, as well as heating and cooling systems.

Scope 3—Here's where the real differentiators emerge, since for most companies the lion's share of emissions resides in scope 3. This measurement spans all greenhouse gas emissions throughout the entire value chain, both upstream and downstream. For instance, when a phone company creates a new smartphone, emissions are generated not only from using the phone during its life, but also from its disposal when it is no longer in use.

Numerous companies that proudly claim carbon neutrality reveal a different story on closer examination. The fine print often reveals that their measurement pertains solely to scope 1 and scope 2 emissions, conveniently overlooking any outsourced carbon-intensive activities. Consequently, we highly advocate considering the collective impact of scopes 1, 2, and 3. Failing to do so renders the provided information essentially meaningless.

Where to find this information?

This framework is basic, but it does have the clear advantage of being, well, basic.[11] Currently it is not mandatory to report on scopes 1, 2, and 3, but with regulation changes coming in the EU, it will become mandatory in the near future. For the companies that already report on it, you can find this information in either their annual report or their ESG report.

Key takeaways

Impact investing can be just as rewarding for all involved as traditional investing. Although there isn't a universally agreed-upon description of impact investing, the diverse frameworks available offer different avenues for gauging its effects.

- **ESG:** This framework helps evaluate and compare companies based on how they contribute positively to society within the areas of environment, social, and governance.
- **The 17 SDGs:** The UN's Sustainable Development Goals seek to end poverty and build a sustainable world. You can pick your favorite goal(s), then find companies who focus on them.
- **SFDR:** The Sustainable Finance Disclosure Regulation divides funds into three different categories based on how sustainable they are. This makes it easier to compare funds.
- **EU Taxonomy:** A classification system for making sustainability reporting more transparent by setting out specific criteria that companies must live up to.
- **Scopes 1, 2, and 3:** This framework measures emissions, but it's not easy for private investors to access the information.

Common dilemmas of *impact investing*

Gray areas of *green investing*

Impact investing is a powerful tool for those who wish to invest their money with purpose and create a positive impact on society and the planet. However, it is not without ethical dilemmas. As investors strive to achieve both financial returns and social impact, they must navigate complex trade-offs, which requires a deeper understanding of the problems and opportunities that come with impact investing. By rising to these challenges, impact investors have the power to create meaningful change and shape a more equitable and sustainable world.

PERFECTION OR TRANSITION?

Dilemma number 1: Should you put your money into companies that are already doing well in terms of ESG, or should you rather support those who are not reaching those targets yet but are working hard to do so?

Impact investing is, of course, all about impact, but it's hard to decide how that is best achieved. On one side, supporting companies that are already doing well seems like a good approach; however, on the other side, an even bigger impact might be achieved by supporting those who are in transition and focusing on change.

Another dimension emerges when comparing a tech company that is achieving carbon neutrality (Perfection) with an energy provider transitioning from conventional to sustainable energy sources (Transition). The question emerges: who is truly making the most substantial mark?

According to the US Governance and Accountability Institute's research, a staggering 92% of S&P 500[1] companies issued sustainability reports in 2021.[2] These reports also outline strategies for improvement (though the effectiveness of these may vary). In investing, cultivating a long-term horizon of at least five years is generally prudent. The strategies outlined in these annual reports could provide insight into a company's trajectory for the next five, ten, or even twenty years.

Impact investors have the power to create meaningful change and shape a more equitable and sustainable world.

MAKING TOUGH CHOICES

Dilemma number 2: There's no such thing as a perfect investment when it comes to impact. Unfortunately, this means you have to compromise because you can't get everything in one. But how do you decide which impact values you are prepared to compromise on?

Finding companies that hit all of the UN's development goals is pretty impossible, because they don't exist. You will find companies that do well in one area but may lag behind on others. Imagine finding a company that's doing excellent work within climate change but the entire leadership team consists of middle-aged, white, straight, cis men. Is it worth supporting a good cause when the people in charge don't include anyone outside their own gender or race? Imagine how that mentality might affect the company culture, not to mention how it contributes to perpetuating the problem of keeping women and ethnic minorities from positions of power. (If you follow our work you know we don't buy the excuse of "there weren't any qualified women or people of color.") You need to decide where you will draw the line.

PRODUCT OR PRODUCTION?

Dilemma number 3: When assessing how a company fits your personal values, there are two things to consider: the product and its production. In other words, would you be happy to invest in a company that follows a perfectly sustainable production process if the product they are offering is fast fashion?

WHO IS THE VOICE OF AUTHORITY?

Dilemma number 4: We've talked a lot about ethics and sustainability, but who actually decides whether a company ticks these boxes? This is an enormous dilemma we could probably fill another 300 pages discussing, but in short, it's complicated.... There are endless opinions about this topic, but no one voice of authority.

The desire for social responsibility has grown so quickly that the infrastructure is struggling to keep up. While the UN's principles have helped add some direction to social responsibility, the figures behind those agendas remain murky. There is no official entity that decides whether a company lives up to impact standards, but plenty of analytics companies (Refinitiv, Morningstar, Bloomberg, and Sustainalytics) have made their own rating systems. Their different ways of defining ethics and sustainability makes it complex for investors to understand, while also enabling sneaky companies to hide behind blurry definitions. Fortunately, the EU is working on legal requirements for large companies, which will make these points easier to compare.

To begin with, you need to decide whether there are industries that you simply want to avoid altogether because the products they produce have a negative environmental or societal impact—thereby making the world a worse place.

When comparing companies in terms of production processes, you need to look at companies within the same industry. It's difficult to compare the output of a tech company with that of, say, a food company, because their operations, processes, and products will be totally different. By only comparing companies within the same industry, it's easier to understand the benchmark.

SUSTAINABLE DILEMMAS IRL

Let's explore real-life examples of companies that have found themselves in ethical dilemmas, and the challenges that investors face when deciding whether to invest in them. By examining these case studies, we can better understand the complexities of impact investing and the importance of doing careful due diligence and maintaining ongoing engagement to ensure that our investments align with our values and promote positive change.

N.B.: When talking through these dilemmas, we will present the stock market and the stock ticker after the company, so that you can do your own research into the stock after pondering each dilemma!

Did you know?

The Corporate Knights (a media and research company focused on advancing a sustainable economy) has listed the 100 most sustainable companies globally. Only five of these had a majority of women on their board and 11 had an equal split. The remaining 84 had a majority of men.[3]

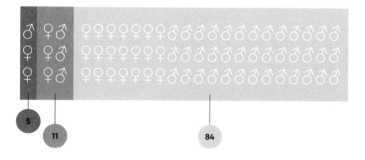

After reading each product versus production dilemma, you might find that a few of the companies we cite as examples in your personal opinion fall short of what constitutes impact. If that's the case, see these examples as a learning opportunity, and refine your ability to gauge a company's genuine impact.

Volkswagen (ETR: VOW3)
Volkswagen was found to have cheated on an emissions test back in 2015 in the US. In short, they installed software that changed how the engine ran during testing to make it look like they weren't polluting as much. In reality, the cars were emitting dangerous pollutants at levels 40 times more than permitted. [4, 5, 6] Since the scandal broke, the company has worked hard to improve their position by launching a series of ambitious sustainability goals.[7]

Dilemma: Once a cheater always a cheater? Should investors continue to support a company that has contributed, and still contributes, so negatively to air pollution, or should they back the (cleaner!) winds of change?

BP (LON: BP)—Originally known as British Petroleum, in recent years this oil and gas power giant has spent millions of dollars rebranding to reflect a more sustainable stance. We present to you: "Beyond Petroleum." However, while launching environmentally friendly initiatives, the company has been heavily criticized for failing to protect workers who have died in oil rig explosions. At the same time, they have also continued activities and exploration into sources for oil, which has resulted in damaging spills in Alaska and the Gulf of Mexico.[8] But—and there is a but—they are one of the world's largest companies, and as such they have the money and power to make serious progress toward a greener future. So even if they just spend a tiny part of their revenue on green initiatives, it has much more impact than anything that smaller companies could ever dream to achieve.

Dilemma: Do you fund companies that have the power to drive change, even though the change still isn't happening as quickly as needed?

We all have the power to change the world—one investment at a time.

Coca-Cola (NYSE: KO)—Around the world, people are familiar with the Coca-Cola brand and its products. However, according to a report by the Changing Markets Foundation, Coca-Cola tries to hide behind misleading marketing when it comes to pollution. The report states that Coca-Cola has spent millions on advertising that its bottles contain 25% marine plastic, without disclosing the fact that it has been found to be the largest producer of plastic pollution in the world.[9] As per the Break Free From Plastic brand audit, Coca-Cola has been the world's worst corporate plastic polluter for five years in a row.[10] This has caused Greenpeace to call out the "blatant greenwashing" by Coca-Cola.[11] The company has also promoted using recycled plastic for its bottles even though less than 10% of all plastic globally is recycled.[12] This means that, regardless of how the plastic is made, 90% of it will eventually break down into microplastics that end up in our air, food, and even in our bodies.[13] The irony? Despite being the world's biggest plastic polluter, Coca-Cola served as a sponsor of the UN Climate Change Conference COP27 in Egypt. Multiple organizations have since condemned this action as greenwashing.[14]

Dilemma: Is Coca-Cola's initiative to recycle plastic a marketing stunt rather than a changemaker, and should investors support it? Is it Coca-Cola's responsibility to encourage recycling in countries where it isn't happening? And should they help find solutions to the problems they've caused, such as reusing existing marine plastics, or should this fall on individual governments across the world?

Hermès (EPA: RMS)—The French luxury fashion brand owns crocodile farms in Australia, from which they get the skin to make their luxury handbags.[15] These farms have been subject to controversy and sparked international outrage. Hermès claim that the crocodiles are well looked after and that they follow science-backed animal welfare methods.[16] Others claim that the welfare policy is irrelevant and that killing any animals for their skins is cruel, inhumane, and, well, unfashionable. Nonetheless, the demand for Hermès crocodile-skin handbags, belts, and shoes continues globally, with big markets in the US and Europe alone. Hermès makes, and the consumer buys.

Dilemma: Is it Hermès' responsibility to stop creating animal-skin handbags if they're in demand and are still being purchased by customers?

H&M (STO: HM-B)—The second-biggest producer of clothes in the world by sales volume, H&M has branded itself as an advocate for conscious and sustainable fashion. This is great, because fashion production is responsible for around 10% of humanity's total carbon dioxide emissions. To put it into perspective, the fashion industry emits more carbon dioxide than all international flights and maritime shipping combined[17]—so finding ways to make the industry more sustainable is long overdue. However, questions have been raised about whether H&M truly lives up to their promise. As a result, the company has been sued over alleged misleading and false sustainability marketing, seeking to capitalize on consumers' interest in sustainable shopping.[18] The fashion giant is also accused of burning 12 tons of unsold garments per year in spite of its ongoing sustainability efforts, although H&M denies these claims.[19]

Dilemma: Are all fast-fashion companies really guilty of being unimpactful or are they trying their best to improve their production methods one step at a time? Should we be investing to further the efforts of those companies who are searching for more sustainable options (even if they themselves are mass polluters at the moment) or should we instead not buy their new clothes and instead put money into finding circular, more immediate solutions to this issue?

Philip Morris International (NYSE: PM)—Philip Morris is one of the world's leading tobacco companies.[20] The Carbon Disclosure Project gave them A ratings in all three of their categories, which are Climate, Forest, and Water Security, one of only 13 companies globally to receive this highest rating in all three of their sustainability categories. But this is for the creation and production of tobacco, a product that kills millions every year.[21]

Dilemma: Tobacco is a product that causes millions of deaths and burdens healthcare systems with the illnesses caused by smoking. So, should their hugely impressive sustainability scores outweigh the damage that they cause to human health?

Key takeaways

Impact investing is (unfortunately) not simple, and you'll find that you constantly need to reprioritize your different values. In this chapter, we've outlined the key dilemmas to consider:

- **Dilemma 1:** Perfect or transitioning? Supporting companies in transition may have a bigger impact in creating change.
- **Dilemma 2:** Making tough choices. Companies may excel in one area but lag behind in others, forcing investors to make difficult trade-offs between their values.
- **Dilemma 3:** Product or production? When assessing a company's fit with your personal values, you need to consider both product and production, keeping in mind that companies may shine in different areas.
- **Dilemma 4:** Who is the voice of authority? Various analytics companies have their own rating systems, adding to the complexity. The EU is working on legal requirements to enhance transparency and comparability in the future.

Following your inner values

3

How to align your inner values with *your investments*

Values represent our foundational beliefs, shaping not only our actions but also our reactions. Every aspect of our lives—the choices we make, the aspirations we nurture, the relationships we form, and the companies we admire—mirror the expression of these core values.

Personal values serve as the very essence of our individuality, though their power is often underestimated. The greater our understanding of our guiding principles, the more confidence we gain in making decisions toward that end.

In this chapter we will explore why values are important, what informs them and how you can figure out what yours are so that you can make decisions that work for you and your money.

Your personal values reflect your past and guide your future.

Your life story is your *biggest asset*

Our values are the sum of our life experiences; they determine our choice of career, our friendships, romantic partners, lifestyle, and goals. They also set the limits on what we believe to be acceptable, fair, and just.

We all have a fundamental personal code that we carry through life, which will become the lens through which we see the world. If you have been a victim of social injustice—be it sexism, racism, or something else—we suspect that equal rights is probably an important value to you.

In the process of educating women in over 100 countries on how to manage their money, we have had front-row seats to the many injustices that have been handed out in relation to the gender wealth gap. We have also seen firsthand how the odds are stacked against women, hitting women from ethnic minorities significantly harder. To say it has lit a fire in us would be an understatement. That's why we've dedicated our time to understanding the roots of the issue—and to finding ways to solve it—using our own experiences as the very fuel that drives us to create change in society. Of course, we're making money through these investments, too, but this ultimately enables us to invest in companies that are attempting to solve important societal issues, thereby creating an even greater impact.

You can do the same—because no matter who you are or where you're from, you'll have witnessed injustice in some form. How did it make you feel? Did it anger you? Good. That feeling will spur you on to learn about the topic in detail, which will in turn help you to make smart decisions about how to solve the problem. Maybe you'll invest in companies working to solve it, or maybe you'll lend money to an organization, start a company yourself, or do something completely different. The important thing is that you do *something*.[1]

A value can
be intrinsic
or it can be
adopted: the
important
thing is that it
is authentic.

The evolution of *values*

Our values are shaped in multiple ways; some are instilled in us from a young age, others are acquired through experience. These values can also change throughout our lives—and they should. As we get older and wiser, or as we enter new stages of our life (moving away from home, starting a family, retiring, etc.) it's likely that we adjust our priorities. However, in a world that's rapidly changing, being able to identify and hold on to our core values is more important than ever.

A value can be intrinsic or it can be adopted: the important thing is that it is authentic. There is no right or wrong when it comes to personal values (within the bounds of basic morality!), but you should be aware of the way in which they influence your perspective. Understanding this will help you to set and achieve long-term goals and make financial decisions that are in line with your beliefs.

Why are personal values important?

1 They help you to set long-term goals.
2 They enable you to prioritize your own ambitions.
3 You can get a better sense of clarity about the present and future.
4 They encourage you to be more assertive and to work hard to achieve your dreams.
5 Having values builds up your resilience during challenging times, since you'll have a deeper motivation to keep going.
6 They make you feel more satisfied with your choices, because you know that they're in alignment with your deeper values.[2]

What about 401(k)s?

Retirement plans such as 401(k)s and pensions are a crucial part of planning for your financial future, to ensure you have the freedom and security you desire when you retire. When investing in either, it's important to think long term. Consider your retirement goals, risk tolerance, and time horizon. When choosing your investments, diversifying them is key, to ensure you spread risk across different asset classes, such as stocks, bonds, and real estate. But don't forget about investing with your values, too. This is especially important for retirement investing, because it's the biggest pool of invested money that most people have. Impact investing for your retirement allows you to support the companies that prioritize ethical practices and sustainable initiatives. This not only provides financial security for your retirement, but also promotes a more inclusive and sustainable future. Your retirement investments can make a meaningful difference in creating the world you want to retire in.

FIVE STEPS TO IDENTIFYING YOUR VALUES

If you're not sure where to start, these steps will help you to find your own personal values and translate them into priorities that you can use to guide your financial decisions.

1 **Identify the biggest priorities in your life right now.** This will help you determine your long-term goals and figure out your time horizon and risk profile. For example, if you plan to buy a home within the next two years, you will probably want to hold off putting your money into investing and instead focus on saving it. But if you're thinking about getting started on boosting your retirement savings, you might want to invest in riskier assets that have a longer time horizon.

2 **What are you excited about?** What gives you butterflies? What makes you want to get started or get involved? This question is wide open, of course, and your answer to it can involve anything from personal relationships to overarching themes, or even the achievements of others.

3 **What is your specific area of expertise?**
Regardless of who you are, where you're from or what you work with, everyone has some area that they know more about than the average person. It could be through knowledge that you acquired while working in your job, or through a hobby that you've studied and practiced passionately. No matter what the area, there will be companies operating within it, and that will give you an advantage when determining which one you want to invest in.

4 **Which societal issues make you angry?**
When used in the right way, anger is a powerful tool to drive change. By identifying the issues that trigger you, you can start finding solutions to these, then research ways to support these solutions with your money, whether that's by investing in companies with a product or service, lending someone money, or helping to crowdfund new ideas.

5 **Group your values into themes.**
Once you've gone through this exercise, it's time to group your findings into overarching themes. You'll most likely find commonalities between what angers and excites you and where your special areas of expertise lie. Once you've identified these themes, you can use them to guide your investment decisions—either by investing in companies that create solutions or by investing in assets that support your long-term goals.

Modern slavery still exists, and *we all have a role in ending it*

First of all, modern slavery is not necessarily the image you might have of people in chains. It can take many forms,[3] including forced labor—work or services that people are forced to do against their will and often under threat of punishment, or debt bondage or bonded labor, which is the world's most widespread form of slavery. This is when people trapped in poverty borrow money and are forced to work to pay off the debt, which ends in a vicious circle of never being able to repay it.

Then there are forced marriages, when someone is married against their will. In addition, trafficking of people for purposes such as forced prostitution, criminality, or organ removal is common, as well as descent-based slavery, which means that people are treated as property and their "slave" status has been passed through generations, not maternal line. Another type of forced labor is domestic servitude.[4] While this is not always counted as slavery, these people often lack legal protection and are particularly vulnerable to abuse. It is estimated that 50 million people were living under forced labor and forced marriages in 2022. This is a 25% increase since 2016. To get an idea of the magnitude of the problem, note that today around 38 million people globally live with AIDS.[5] The bad news doesn't stop here, because the situation keeps getting worse, as women and girls make up the majority of modern slavery victims. And to make matters even worse, out of the 50 million people living in modern slavery, over 12 million are children.[6] The actual number of people affected by modern slavery might be much higher.

It's important to note that modern slavery can happen anywhere—there have even been cases of sweatshops in Los Angeles, California.[7] But what can we do about it? Aside from supporting organizations that fight modern slavery actively, you as a consumer and investor can make sure that not a single cent lands in the hands of people and companies profiting from modern slaves. Stop buying their products, and absolutely don't invest in them.

So the next time you are looking at buying a dress for 5 dollars from a store, ask yourself the question, how is this possible?

Women and girls make up the majority of modern slavery victims ... out of the 50 million people living in modern slavery, over 12 million are children.

1 What are your priorities?

_____

_____

_____

_____

_____

2 What gives you butterflies?

_____

_____

_____

_____

_____

Your values are the sum of your life experiences.

3 What are your areas of expertise?

_____

_____

_____

_____

4 Which issues anger you?

_____

_____

_____

_____

5 What are the common themes?

_____

_____

_____

_____

_____

Your personal values will influence how you invest, as well as how you set your financial goals.

MARRYING YOUR VALUES WITH YOUR MONEY

When it comes to making financial decisions, most people lean on the advice of others. But what if there was a way to figure out your own financial plan based on your personal values? Contrary to popular belief, personal values are not just a soft concept that impacts your relationships; in fact, they also play a major role in shaping your financial behavior. Quite simply, your personal values will influence how you choose to invest, as well as how you set your financial goals.

Your personal values can help you decide which investments are right for you; whether you're looking for risky investments that have high earnings potential or stable investments for uncertain times, investing based on values can provide the security and peace of mind that you need.

Your faith might also influence how and where you wish to place your money. If you are, for example, Christian, Jewish, or atheist, religious views typically have minimal impact on your investment strategy, because companies are usually relatively neutral in their stance on religion. But you might want to screen specific choices that raise issues for you such as pharmaceutical companies that produce contraceptive products, or arms companies developing weapons, depending on your denomination of these religions. In most cases these decisions come down to personal beliefs rather than religious guidance.

FIVE STEPS TO MATCHING YOUR VALUES WITH COMPANIES

You've identified the issues that matter most to you, so now it's time to find the companies that share your values and are working on issues to solve them.

1 **Research and identify.** Research companies on the major stock exchange in your country. For example, if you're in the US, explore the S&P 500 (the 500 biggest companies on the stock exchange) and assess how their sustainability credentials matchthe 17 UN goals.

2 **Assess values and strength.** Refine your list by removing companies that don't match your values and adding missing companies that you find particularly impactful. Consider using color-codes to prioritize your values and categorize companies accordingly.

3 **Verify Values and Build Portfolio.** Examine each company's annual and sustainability reports based on the ESG framework. Verify their commitment to societal and environmental concerns. Once you find financially sound companies aligned with your values, compile a working list of potential investments, highlighting how each meets your values.

In subsequent chapters we will take you through how to assemble a financially sound portfolio and how to conduct your own due dilligence.

Your personal values are shaped by your past experiences, and these impact every aspect of your future.

FAITH-BASED INVESTING

If you practice a religion such as Christianity, Judaism, or Islam, you may want to look into faith-based investing. This will ensure that your financial decisions are in line with the principles of your faith.

Depending on the religion, there can be strict rules to investment. However, for all, the one central part is to ensure that whatever a company is producing and doing complies with any of a faith's central beliefs.

In the US for example, major investment firms such as Morgan Stanley are well versed in helping steer clients of major faiths toward companies that are in line with their clients' religious beliefs and values. There are also many faith-based firms focused solely on specific religions. These firms focus on everyone from Catholics to Buddhists.

There are also specific religious laws or guidelines that affect some types of relgious investment. For example, if you are a practicing Jew, you may want to be guided by general Jewish principles such as avoiding high-risk investment, which could be seen as a form of gambling. If you are a Muslim, you may want to make your investments Sharia law compliant. This would ensure that your investments go to companies that are actively improving society. Certain sectors would therefore be off limits, including alcohol, arms, and pornography.

It's possible to align your investments with your religious beliefs.

Key takeaways

Your personal values are shaped by your past experiences, and these impact every aspect of your future. By identifying and then prioritizing your personal values, you can make investment decisions that align with your beliefs:

- **Steps to identify personal values** include prioritizing your life goals, identifying your passions, reflecting which social issues you care most about and grouping your values into themes.
- **Religious beliefs** can guide investment choices for some individuals.
- **Matching your values** with your investments is a powerful tool to create positive change while making money.

Investing
basics

4

Crash course in investing

According to a study by Merrill Lynch, 61% of women say they'd rather discuss their own death than talk about their money.[1] Discussions around money are often sensitive, but that needs to change—money is power and women need to take back that power for themselves.

This book is not an introduction to investing—for that information you want to buy our first book, *Girls Just Wanna Have Funds—A Feminist Guide to Investing.* So we won't go through all the basics of the stock market and how it works here. However, there are a few key things you should understand before you decide on your investment portfolio, and we'll outline these in this chapter. Knowing these will make investing simpler, but it will also make it much easier to navigate the landscape of impact investing.

61% of women say they'd rather discuss their own death than talk about their money.

THE
FUNDAMENTALS

No matter what you decide to invest in, first you need to understand a few basic topics and terms.

Time horizon

This expression refers to the length of time for which you will keep your investments. Historically, being a long-term investor has been a winning strategy (especially if you diversify), and in order to qualify as such, you need a time horizon of at least five years (but preferably much longer).

Compound interest

Compound interest is what makes investing truly life-changing over time. Simply put, this is the concept of making profit off your profit over a period of time. For example: you invest $100 in the stock market. Within the first year, your investment increases by 10%, equivalent to $10. The value of your investment is now $110 and you keep it for another year without changing anything. Next year, your investment increases by 10% again, and now that is equivalent to $11 because you're also making money off last year's gain ($110 total). In this way, the value of your investment will accelerate over time as you earn money on both the initial investment and the growing return.

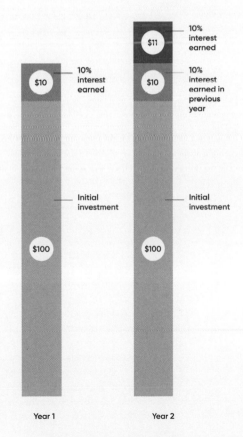

$10 — 10% interest earned

$11 — 10% interest earned

$10 — 10% interest earned in previous year

Initial investment

Initial investment

$100

$100

Year 1

Year 2

Risk

Every investment involves some degree of risk, and it's commonly said that risk and reward go hand in hand. This means that the riskier the investment, the bigger the potential return.

There are two types of risk:

- **Market risk:** These are risks that apply to every company in the market, such as pandemics, war, and global economic downturns.
- **Company risk:** These are risks that only apply to the specific company, such as new legislation affecting that company or its business, suppliers going bankrupt, or new competitors entering the market.

Diversification

Diversification is the concept of spreading out your risk by investing in a lot of different things. This could be different stocks (preferably at least 10 to 20) but it also could be different asset classes, which we'll cover on page 94 in this book.

Balancing out risk

Having a blend of sectors, geographical regions, and sizes of companies helps to balance out the risk of a hit in one of those areas. Another way to mix it up is by investing in asset classes that react differently to changes in the economy. One such example is bonds, because when the interest rate increases, the return on bonds increases, whereas most stocks are negatively impacted. This will all make sense later in the book (see pages 87–90).

CONSIDERATIONS WHEN PICKING INVESTMENTS

For most people, identifying the right investments for them feels overwhelming. Life would be much easier if only there was a simple recipe for how to choose the best ones. Even though there's no certainty that can be given when you choose an investment, we've outlined three aspects to consider:

1 Look at the economy

The global economy moves between cycles of economic upturn and downturn. When the economy is growing, people are optimistic about the future and their finances and they have more money to spend. However, in times of economic downturn and uncertainty, most people are more reluctant to spend money.

These tendencies are reflected in the stock market, which usually follows changes in the overall economy. However, not all stocks react in the same way to changes in the economy, and this is also true of bonds, funds, and alternative investments, even though different groups of assets may react differently to changes in the economy.

We'll use stocks here to explain how these differences can arise:

- **Cyclical stocks:** Cyclical companies produce non-essential products that people tend to splurge on when things are going well. This could be jewelry, clothing, or travel. Therefore, these companies tend to follow fluctuations in the overall economy—doing well when the economy is booming and struggling during times of crisis.

- **Non-cyclical stocks:** Non-cyclical companies, on the other hand, produce essential things like food and medicine, which people will buy regardless of their financial situation. As a result, these companies are less vulnerable to economic fluctuations, and they tend to perform better in times of crisis. These stocks are also known as "defensive stocks," because they can be a potential line of defense when markets are falling.

Having a long time horizon is key to becoming a successful investor.

Think long term

Having a long time horizon is key to becoming a successful investor, so when picking what to invest in, it's a good idea to consider what products/services/assets you think might be in demand in the future. If you can successfully predict future needs, you're likely to make a good profit.

At the same time, consider your life situation—do you have any big changes coming up (getting married/divorced, having kids, retiring, buying a home)?—and use this to guide your time horizon.

Use your own experience

Choosing investments based on your own experience with them might seem too easy, but it's actually a good approach. The great thing about investing in brands you know and love is that you are confident in the product—and the chance of others feeling the same way is maybe higher compared to investing in a product you don't like or understand. This is a really useful approach, because every time you go out to the supermarket, eat out, or walk around, you are potentially scouting investment opportunities.

Key takeaways

To get the most out of this book, a basic understanding of investing is needed, which is covered in our first book, *Girls Just Wanna Have Funds—A Feminist Guide to Investing*, but this chapter covers the most important concepts.

- **Time horizon** of at least five years is recommended for long-term investing.
- **Compound interest** allows for profit to accelerate over time.
- **Risk** can be divided into two types: market risk (the risks of the overall stock market) and company risk (risks specifically affecting individual companies).
- **Diversification** is the concept of spreading out your risk by investing in different things. As a rule of thumb, you need to invest in at least 10 different stocks to have a diversified portfolio. Diversification can also be achieved by investing in funds or different asset types.

Mainstream
investing

5

Stocks, funds, and bonds

Many of us are lucky enough to now go through an education system for at least a decade of our lives. We get taught all sorts of exciting things—from chemistry to history, literature to sports. However, most of us go through the school system without ever learning how to manage our money. This has huge implications and it impacts every aspect of our future.

So how big is this problem? According to the OECD, about half of the EU adult population does not have a good enough understanding of basic financial concepts.[1] These numbers hide a large disparity, because financial illiteracy is much more widespread among women and low-income groups.[2] As a result, the financial world remains open mainly to those who build it and already benefit from it.

This is not just a problem for the individual, it's a problem for society as a whole. This is because financial literacy forms the basis of making informed decisions—not just for yourself, but for society. Investing is like voting with your money; every time you invest in a company, you support that company and help drive up the stock price. Imagine if investors refused to invest in companies that didn't live up to their values? The world would probably look very different then.

THE MAINSTREAM OPTIONS

Before we dive into the mainstream options of impact investing, we need to understand what investing actually is. If you've read our first book *Girls Just Wanna Have Funds —A Feminist Guide to Investing*, or if you're already a member of Female Invest, you might already know much of this, but for everyone else, let's go through the basics.

In short, the term *investing* describes buying something in the hope that it will increase in value over time. You can invest in a lot of different things —from cars and houses to stocks and funds. This chapter will cover stocks, funds, and bonds, all of which are popular choices among both private and professional investors. You'll learn what each asset type is and we'll do our best to give you the tools so that you feel confident to pick some that match your values and have the potential to increase your wealth at the same time.

Did you know?

If you own stocks in a company, you can vote on certain issues within it. However, as an individual investor your impact will be very small. Therefore, it's exciting to see that some organizations start pooling shareholders' votes on specific issues to put pressure on companies to take more impact decisions. The platform Tulipshare is a great example of this collaboration between companies and investors to meet ESG targets. For example, investors have lobbied Coca-Cola to reduce their plastic waste through the platform. By being a shareholder and using that position to come together with others, your investment has the power to unite and drive change from within.[3]

STOCKS

Stocks, also known as equity, are a security that represents ownership of a company. When you buy stocks, you buy a small part of the company that has issued them. This can be a powerful way to promote causes you care about, because when you invest your money in a company, you are essentially helping that company spread its influence and message. A company's success and ability to stay in business is reliant on its stock price, and the money you invest is a reflection of the goals and values that are important to you. As the company then increases (or decreases) in value, so does the value of your investment. Stocks are a popular choice among both private and professional investors for the following reasons:

- You can get started using just small amounts (down to $100).
- There are good historic returns (the historical average annual return is 10% per year).
- They are liquid assets (it often takes only seconds to make a trade).

Stocks are traded on the stock exchange, which works just like any other marketplace. When demand for a certain thing goes up, so does the price. Most countries have their own stock exchange, and if you trade during its opening hours, your trade will often be executed within seconds, which makes stock a highly liquid asset.

You can make money from stocks in two ways:

Value increase: The stock increases in value, and you sell it at a profit.

Dividends: This is when a company pays out part of its profit to its investors. It's worth noting that the stock price often decreases by the same amount as the dividend.

What impacts the stock price

We can't talk about stocks without discussing how their price is determined. While there are many opinions on this, we like to divide this into three different categories.

1 **Company performance:** This covers everything within the company that it can control itself. How good is the leadership team? How efficient are their employees? How good is the product/service the company is selling? The price of a stock does not just reflect past performance, it also reflects an investor's expectations of future performance.

2 **Macroeconomic trends:** Companies are heavily impacted by the world around them, which is outside their control. This could be the overall financial situation, natural disasters, pandemic, legislation, etc.

3 **Investor psychology:** A stock is never worth more than the next investor is willing to pay for it. This is because people aren't always rational, and investor psychology is often impacted by emotions, media, and public opinion.

When Kylie Jenner's tweet cost Snapchat $1.3 billion

On February 12, 2018, Kylie Jenner wrote a tweet saying *"sooo does anyone else not open Snapchat anymore? Or is it just me ... ugh this is so sad."*[16] That day, Snapchat's shares fell by 6%, causing the company to lose $1.3 billion in value. Nothing changed within the company that day: it didn't fire any employees, their headquarters didn't burn down. But that one tweet changed investors' perception of the company and made them lose confidence in it as an investment opportunity. This is a great example of how investor psychology can directly impact stock prices.

What to expect

Historically, investing in stocks has been a good way to build wealth. In fact, the stock market has given an average return of 10% per year (not adjusted for inflation)[5], which by far outperforms keeping your money in the bank.[6] As with all types of investing, stocks hold a certain level of risk and there are no guarantees.

The table below shows the development of the S&P 500 Index (the 500 largest companies in the US), which is commonly used to reflect the overall stock market. Even though returns vary greatly over time, the numbers are strong.

The difference between stocks and shares

The term "stocks" is used to describe ownership of companies in general, while the term "shares" is used to describe ownership of a specific company. Let's take an example: "Tania likes to invest in stocks and she has just bought shares in Netflix."

5-, 10-, 20-, and 30-year Returns on the Stock Market

	Average rate of return	Inflation-adjusted return
5-year (2017-2021)	18.55%	15.19%
10-year (2012-2021)	16.58%	14.15%
20-year (2002-2021)	9.51%	7.04%
30-year (1992-2021)	10.66%	8.10%

TAKING STOCK TO CHANGE THE WORLD

While many people have heard about stocks, most people aren't aware of the power they hold when investing in them.

Investing with your values using stocks is not as simple as it may seem and as we know, there's no such thing as the "perfect company" that lives up to every single value you may have. To make it easier to navigate, there are broadly two things to consider when you're looking to invest sustainably in stocks:

Sustainable product: What the company produces actively aims at improving the future of our planet and potentially reversing negative climate change effects.

Sustainable production: The goods or services that are produced by the company are created in a sustainable fashion.

Going further for sustainability

Patagonia (a private company) is renowned for its sustainable ethos and mission. While you could argue that the production of more clothes isn't great for the planet, Patagonia has made huge strides in taxing themselves for the benefit of the Earth by donating to environmental funds, participating in the rewilding of national parks, and repairing and re-wearing their products.[7] Most recently, the founder of Patagonia, Yvon Chouinard, pledged to give his company to a trust so that all future profits will be donated to climate change-related charities. The mission, rather than the product, is what makes the company a sustainable choice, and boy it's a powerful one.

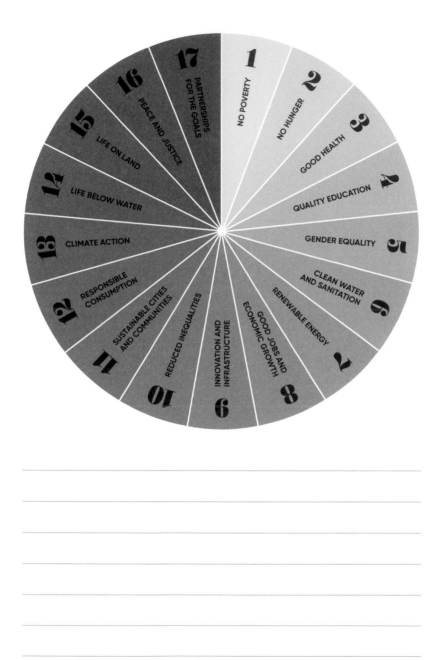

THE SUSTAINABILITY STOCK PIE

You're considering which companies to invest in, but how do you choose? Are you feeling a bit paralyzed by indecision? We're not surprised, we certainly felt like that, too! So let's wind back.

In earlier chapters we've looked at checklists and prioritized what is important to you within the sustainability topic. Now it's time to come back to those 17 UN principles and introduce the concept of the pie to your strategy. We don't mean eating the tasty pastry goodness (although you could do this at the same time), but rather using a pie-shaped strategy to help filter out your choices.

Sustainability stock pie

First, go back to the companies you investigated in Chapter 3, which correspond to and reflect your values. Using the pie opposite, allocate each company to a different area, based on what you think is their main hitting point on the sustainability front. Then start to compile your pie...

Step 1: Look at the companies on a financial index of choice, starting with the one in your country, for example S&P 500 or FTSE 100.

Step 2: Assess each company for a sustainable product or process, and decide whether to dump them or continue with the categorization.

Pick your slice

As you work your way through assessing each stock, you'll start to find that you can clearly put them into one slice of the pie. In an ideal world, you'd invest in stock from each slice of the pie, to have access to all areas of sustainability.

However, unless you've got large amounts of money to invest, it's likely that you'll have to choose between various investments, as we simply cannot afford everything in this life. This is where we come back to the prioritization schedule; you can start to pick the stocks from the pie that most align with your morals. Nonetheless, it's crucial to emphasize that a narrower investment strategy reduces diversification, resulting in a higher level of risk within your portfolio. If you're new to investing or have limited funds, it's advisable to complement your investments in individual impact stocks with allocations to funds or ETFs, as discussed in the following section.

Step 3: Decide which slice of the UN's sustainability pie each company fits into based on what their main focus for sustainability is. There can be overlap and they can fall into more than one if you wish!

Step 4: Continue assessing each company until your pie is looking pretty full. If you feel confident, you could perhaps move on to some other indexes to get some exposure to international stocks or smaller companies.

Step 5: Take a look at your prioritization list to work out which areas of sustainability from the pie are most important to you.

Step 6: Look at the stocks in the most important slice of the pie. Begin to filter them by ranking them on their sustainability credentials that we discussed in Chapter 3.

Step 7: Assess your budget and work out how many stocks you can afford to leap into and which sustainability strategy you might be following (see page 52 for further help!).

Step 8: Carry out further analysis on the companies that are tickling your fancy, to check their underlying company strength.

Step 9: Weigh up the relative sustainability and company accounts of the stocks that you've filtered down in your pie.

Step 10: Purchase those stocks!

Addressing parts of the pie

Burberry Group, a well-known luxury fashion brand, is currently listed on the FTSE 100 and is a good example of a company that isn't perfect but is trying to address its sustainability impact. Burberry does not do well in terms of environmental impact, because of the nature of the products, their constant production, and a lack of recycling of materials, but if we look at other aspects of the company we might see more positives. For example, the founder of Burberry, Thomas Burberry, was a renowned altruist who regularly funded young people in the community, particularly those from under-represented backgrounds. Burberry has continued this legacy into today and has partnerships with charities that give to young people.[8] So if you were assessing this company for the pie, you might put it into the education bracket.

There's no such thing as the "perfect company" that lives up to every single value you may have.

Investment funds

Investment funds are a concept whereby many investors pool their money together. This pool of money is then invested in lots of different things, such as stocks, property, or something else. The way it works is that each fund has a theme and the fund is invested within that theme. When investing in a fund, you invest in all of the things in the fund, which gives you a nice diversification of risk. Pooling your money with other people does mean that you can access an awful lot more investments than you'd be able to individually. Often funds have anything from two to 200-plus investments within them.

To make it clear what the fund is up to, they state their themes quite clearly in their name and strategy sheet (called a KIID). It might be that it invests in a specific geographical region, such as China, or in a specific sector, such as pharmaceuticals. They can also vary in the size of companies they go for—such as small, medium, or Big Corp—and there are funds out there that branch beyond stocks and shares and hold other investments, too, such as commodities, property, and even collectibles.

When considering funds, it's worth knowing and understanding the key differences between the two main ways of structuring them—active and passive.

ACTIVE FUNDS

Active funds have a hired Fund Manager who will buy and sell on behalf of the fund, usually with a team of analysts to help with the goal of outperforming the overall market. This option is usually pricier than a passive fund, because man and woman power costs money.

Pro:
- More specific investment areas to cater to investors' desires.

Con:
- Higher costs—the knowledge and expertise has to be compensated.

PASSIVE FUNDS

Passive funds do not hire anyone to update their investments. Instead, the bank or financial institution making the fund decides what should be in it on the day it is made, then they never change it again. The goal is to keep costs low, follow the market, and get the average market return. These funds often follow an index.

Pro:
- Lower cost—there is only a computer doing the work.

Con:
- Performance—they will only ever match the market.

ETFs

Exchange-traded funds (ETFs) are a type of investment fund designed to track the performance of a particular index, such as the S&P 500 or the NASDAQ. ETFs can hold a variety of assets, such as stocks, bonds, and commodities, and expose investors to a diversified portfolio of assets.

ETFs are different from active and passive funds in their management style. Passive funds, such as index funds, seek to replicate the performance of a particular index and have lower fees because they are not actively managed. In contrast, active funds are managed by a portfolio manager who selects individual stocks or bonds to try to outperform the market.

The main difference with ETFs is that they are traded on an exchange and their price can fluctuate throughout the day. This makes ETFs more flexible than traditional funds, which are priced once a day after the market closes. Additionally, ETFs have lower fees than actively managed funds because they require less active management. This makes ETFs an increasingly popular investment choice.

Bonds

It's commonly said that bonds are the opposite of stocks, because while you get ownership from buying stocks, you give out a loan when buying bonds. In this way, bonds are essentially a loan from you as the investor to either a large company or a government. As a thank you for lending them money, the borrower usually pays a rate of interest, which is a key benefit of bonds because it is a form of income. For most bonds, this takes place throughout the duration of the loan, although this can vary slightly. The time period for individual bonds is set out at the beginning of the bond, after which the money you initially lent will be returned.[9]

The amount of interest that bonds pay depends on two things: the length of time of the loan and the reliability of the borrower. Generally speaking, bonds that have a longer duration will pay higher interest rates, because there is more risk that over time conditions will change and so the borrower needs to compensate for that. Tying into the idea of risk, if the borrower is seen as a more risky option—in other words, there's a chance that they won't be able to pay you back the money you've lent—then they will pay more interest to compensate for that insecurity.

The 60/40 rule

The 60/40 rule is a popular concept when interest rates are high, because this is when bonds become an attractive option. Following this rule, investors put 60% of their money into stocks and 40% into bonds. This strategy offers the upside of the stock market and the safety of bonds. While this strategy has been popular among investors for decades, it gave the worst returns in 100 years in 2022.

Did you know?

While bonds are often considered more stable, less sexy, and less exciting versions of stocks, the global market for bonds is actually bigger in size than the stock market.[10] Another interesting fact about bonds is that bond prices are inversely correlated with interest rates: When interest rates go up, bond prices fall and vice-versa. [11, 12]

Bonds all get a credit rating that should help to let us know how risky they might be, which comes from agencies like Moody's, Standard & Poor, and Fitch. They give ratings all the way from investment grade to junk (a bond given the lowest credit rating—for example, for companies that are new or have had financial difficulties and therefore may be more of a risk for repayment). You might've deduced by now that junk grade bonds pay the highest rate of interest, but, as the name suggests, they're so risky that analysts deem them unattractive. From these ratings you can also assess various other points, such as how sustainable the borrower is and what they might be doing with the money that's being lent.

Despite the junk bonds, overall, bonds are seen to be a less risky investment than stocks and their main benefit is the income that they can generate. In the same way that stocks list on an IPO (Initial Public Offering), bonds first hit the market as they're released. The amount of money required to buy bonds at this stage is usually quite high, so it's often only the big banks, other governments, and investment funds who are getting involved. After this, bonds can be bought from those that got in there first—either in the form of a pure bond, or in funds that bundle multiple bonds together. As the world wakes up to needing to be more sustainable if we want to have a planet for the next generation, "green" bonds have started popping up and are becoming ever more popular. More on them on the opposite page!

HOW TO HAVE AN IMPACT WITH BONDS

Bonds have a reputation of being low risk and low reward, which is why most people don't get excited about them. However, the market for bonds is becoming increasingly captivating as interest rates are increasing, because the yield of bonds tends to follow the interest rate and thereby increase in times when interest rates increase. At the same time, new types of bonds have started to emerge, some of which offer the opportunity to make the world a better place. So let's look at the two main types: Green bonds and Orange bonds.

Green goes global

The World Bank is a major issuer of Green bonds and issued $14.4 billion of them between 2008 and 2020. The money has been used to support 111 projects around the world, mainly within renewable energy, clean transportation, and agriculture.[16] On a national level, in 2019 Sweden set an example for future government and corporate bonds as the first country to launch a purely green government bond. Nonetheless, it's crucial to emphasize that a narrower investment strategy reduces diversification, resulting in a higher level of risk within your portfolio. If you're new to investing or have limited funds, it's advisable to complement your investments in individual impact stocks with allocations to funds or ETFs, as discussed in the following section.

Green bonds

What it is: Green bonds fund projects that deliver clear environmental benefits, such as renewable energy or biodiversity conservation.[13] With a rapidly growing demand for renewable energy, this is where Green bonds come into play. Selling these bonds raises money for new and existing projects that focus on environmental benefits and a more sustainable economy. Bond issuances (excluding Green bonds) can be used by companies for financing purposes as they desire. Funds from Green bonds, on the other hand, are utilized for a specific purpose. An example could be that Chile issues a government bond to finance their budget deficit or a general project (such as establishing hospitals). Chile could also issue a green bond with the specific purpose of establishing a wind farm or transitioning bus operations from diesel-powered to electric buses. Therefore, Green bonds are also known as "climate bonds."[14] A small distinction to note is that if you buy Green bonds through an ETF or fund, this will be Green bonds that have already been issued, known as the secondary market. You're therefore not directly financing the production of green energy, but purchasing the right to collect the interests. The influence of purchasing the bond in the primary market is significant, whereas acquiring the bond in the secondary market holds minimal impact.

How to buy them: Even though most investments in Green bonds are made by institutional investors (big companies), there are also options to get involved as a private investor. As a private investor, the best way to buy Green bonds is through funds, or ETFs. One example is the iShares USD Green Bond ETF, which follows the performance of a group of bonds used to finance environmental projects.[15]

Orange bonds

What it is: Orange bonds work in much the same way as Green bonds, but instead of financing projects within green energy, Orange bonds are used to finance projects in support of women and girls. Why orange? Because orange is the color of the UN Sustainable Development Goal 5: Gender Equality. Orange bonds are the world's first gender-lens-investing asset class, which essentially means it's the first ever type of investment that specifically seeks to benefit women and girls.

How to buy them: Orange bonds were released in October 2022, so they are still a very new concept and are not, unfortunately, available to private investors yet. However, we absolutely love the concept and we hope that they will soon be accessible through funds and ETFs, just like green bonds.

An estimated 100 million women and girls are expected to benefit from orange bonds by 2030.[17]

Key takeaways

Stocks, funds, and bonds are popular choices among private investors, and they all offer plenty of room for investing with your values.

- **Stocks:** When identifying stocks that match your values, you can focus on either product or production.
- **Funds:** A nice tool for diversification, because each fund contains many different investments. Most trading platforms offer sustainability ratings for funds.
- **Bonds:** Offering lower volatility and lower returns, bonds can complement stocks well. Impact options include Green and Orange bonds.

How to invest beyond the mainstream

Diversifying your portfolio

In the previous chapter we explained that stocks, funds, and bonds are common choices for private investors. However, a great way to spread your risk is by diversifying your portfolio with asset classes that fall outside the norm. These are collectively referred to as "alternative investments" and they cover a large category of different investment options. Many alternative investments are not relevant for private investors, because they require significant capital or highly specialized knowledge. This includes categories such as private equity and venture capital, which is dominated by institutional investors. There are alternative investment opportunities that are available to private investors. These options span a wide range, encompassing everything from art to commodities. In this chapter, we will discuss the asset classes that we consider to hold significant potential for creating an impact.

1 **Crowdfunding:** Investing smaller amounts in startups alongside many other investors.

2 **Crypto:** Buying digital currencies which often exist on decentralized networks using blockchain technology (don't worry, we'll explain).

3 **Angel investing:** Investing bigger amounts in startups alongside fewer other investors.

4 **Property:** We'll cover four ways to invest in property, depending on your time horizon, risk level, and how much money you have.

As you will learn throughout this chapter, the capital requirement, risk, and liquidity will be very different for each of these asset classes. It's also important to note that the potential for having a positive impact through these investments will vary greatly. A lot of research has been done on this—and the results of different studies may vary. In many ways, this underlines the complexity of measuring and defining true impact. When writing this book, we've done our best to give you the tools you need to make educated decisions for yourself.

A great way to spread your risk is by diversifying your portfolio with asset classes that fall outside the norm.

Crowdfunding

As you know, when you invest in stocks, you often invest in very large companies, which, for most, will result in just a tiny share of ownership. But what if you want to support a smaller company that isn't yet listed on the stock exchange? Or support the development of an idea you really believe in? This is where crowdfunding can offer an alternative. Simply put, crowdfunding is a way to bring together money from lots of people to fund a specific business with a cause or product that is particularly promising.[1]

Before we dive into the three different types of crowdfunding, we need to understand why new companies seek to raise money in the first place. Starting a business can be expensive; hiring people, building a product/service, and doing research all require capital. Depending on the type of company, building a business can easily take years and cost millions. Prior to the rise of crowdfunding, it was almost exclusively big institutions called venture capital funds, wealthy "angels" (more on them later), or those with huge amounts of money and connections that could invest in new businesses.[2] Gaining funding as a new business usually requires access to networks of ultra-wealthy individuals.

According to a 2023 *Harvard Business Review* publication, the field of venture capital predominantly favors men, resulting in significant under-representation of women in both venture-backed entrepreneurship and VC investment roles. The article reveals that companies founded exclusively by women receive a mere 2% of all venture capital investments, while women make up less than 15% of VC investors. This gender disparity creates a self-perpetuating cycle: since venture capitalists tend to prefer investing in individuals who resemble them, it's not surprising that male-led startups receive more funding, as most investors are male themselves.[3]

Does it bother you that women and people of color barely receive funding? If it does, good. It's absolutely outrageous to see numbers like this well into the twenty-first century. But fear not, crowdfunding is one potential solution, as it gives women, people of color, other minority groups, and underfunded entrepreneurs the opportunity to fund their business. Investors can get involved with as little as $10,[4] joining forces with others to give businesses the money they need. The best part? If the company continues to grow and do well, your investment will increase in value, too.

In 2022, only around 2% of traditional venture capital funding went to female-led startups, while black founders received just 1% of capital.

Did you know?

In 2022, only around 2% of traditional venture capital funding went to female-led startups, while black founders received just 1% of capital.[5, 6] Yes, you read that right! This constitutes a MAJOR democratic problem, because founders often solve problems they experience themselves, while investors fund solutions to problems they can relate to. When women and people of color are under-represented on both sides of the table, their ideas are never brought to life.

CROWDFUNDING BASICS

Let's briefly go through the three types of crowdfunding that are available and identify the one that can be used as an investment.

1 **Donation-based crowdfunding**
   As you would expect, this is basically a coordinated donation and not an investment, as you do not get anything in return —except lots of good karma for your charity!

2 **Reward-based crowdfunding**
   In this case you will receive some sort of perk or reward as a thank you for investing. This will often be closely linked to the business in question, such as a discount on the product they are making. However, as you do not get your money back, we are reluctant to call this an investment.

3 **Equity-based crowdfunding**
   This type of crowdfunding works just like investing in stocks on the stock exchange: you invest money and in return you get some ownership of the company. When the company increases in value, the value of your shares increases with it.

We will focus mostly on equity-based crowdfunding examples throughout this chapter as it's the type of crowdfunding that allows investors to put their money somewhere to improve the world AND gain a return on their cash. Sounds good, right?

Origin story

The modern wave of crowdfunding emerged in Amsterdam, with a platform called SellaBand, which focused purely on helping musicians and artists get their work off the ground. More than 85% of investors came from over 60 miles away from each individual running the pitch, which showed how far online crowdfunding branches could reach. Kickstarter quickly followed in the US, launching all three types of crowdfunding and more opportunities in different sectors than it could be possible to count.[7] And it's been so successful, it just keeps growing. During 2011, the UK saw only eight crowdfunding launches on accessible platforms, while 10 years later, in 2021, there were 537.[8]

During 2011, the UK saw only eight crowdfunding launches on accessible platforms, while 10 years later, in 2021, there were 537.

WHAT YOU NEED TO KNOW

Although equity-based crowdfunding and investing in stocks are in many ways similar, there are a few key distinctions you need to be aware of:

1 **Timing**—Companies at this stage only crowdfund when they need more money. This means there is a set period of time in which you can invest in their crowdfund. How often a company fundraises varies, but this will typically be no more than once a year for a set period of a few weeks. Once the funding round is closed, it's done, and you've missed your chance, unless the company decides to crowdfund again at a later stage.

2 **Research**—Doing your own research is always key, but with small or new companies it is much harder to get the information and details you need, so due diligence on both the financials and ethics of the company is more challenging (see Chapter 7 for more info on how to do this). Note that crowdfunding has a high risk attached to the potential for a high reward.

3 **Selling**—Stocks listed on a stock exchange are very liquid, meaning it's typically easy to buy and sell at any given time. There is often very little possibility to sell a crowdfunding investment, as there are relatively few established marketplaces for it, and even fewer willing buyers. Sometimes your investment may need to be held onto for a set number of years or until the company gets bought or goes public (IPO). This means you have to be sure you won't need the money that you invested back for at least a few years.

Tax benefits—Investing in crowdfunding can come with certain tax perks that traditional stocks and shares don't have. The US, UK, Spain, Germany, and France are among the few countries that incentivize investors to put their money into startup companies.[9]

4 **Consider risk**—It's crucial to investigate the motivation behind a company's crowdfunding—why a company opts for this approach over conventional funding avenues like bank loans or venture capital. This decision could stem from the company's desire to engage

customers as investors and cultivate brand advocates (as demonstrated effectively by notable cases like Chip and Brewdog). Conversely, it might be due to challenges encountered while seeking funding from other sources. Additionally, bear in mind that given the generally modest scale of crowdfunding enterprises, the associated risk tends to be considerably greater compared to publicly traded companies on the stock exchange.

The potential impact

Crowdfunding is an exciting way to invest in smaller companies that have not yet been listed on the stock exchange, but how can you make an impact with your crowdfunding investment? And, crucially, how is it actually going to benefit those who receive it?

Social impact

This is one of the most impactful ways by which you can support young, up-and-coming businesses, but crowdfunding also puts the power in your hands to support female-led, minority-led, and diverse teams that you believe deserve funding. Even better news is that female-led crowdfunded businesses have proven to be a safer bet, with a more successful track record than male-led ones,

despite the relatively low levels of funding received.

Below are a few examples of companies that have previously crowdfunded, to give you an idea of the impact you can expect.

Nc'nean whisky: Nc'nean is an organic, sustainable whisky business that started on a crowdfunding platform. The founder, Annabel Thomas, quit her London job, raised €1.9 million[10] and began distilling whisky in West Scotland. The company recycles 99.97% of their waste, and they bottle their product into recycled glass, which is an industry first.[11] A successful crowdfunding campaign by a female founder, in a remote region, with a sustainable product? Who said you couldn't have it all!

Yoni: This female-led startup from the Netherlands wants to revolutionize the fem-care industry, and focuses on sustainable period products. In 2022 they raised €1.2 million via crowdfunding from over 450 investors, helping them to expand their business. If Yoni is successful, these investors could make a decent return even by having a small share of that young company. How well Yoni will perform and how decent the return will be remains to be seen.

HOW CAN I GET INVOLVED – AND SHOULD I?

Crowdfunding puts your money into the businesses you'd like to see grow in the future. There's no guarantee that they'll make it, though, as starting out is notoriously difficult and comes with many curveballs. Around 70% of startups fail within their first five years of operations, making them a risky investment.[12] Some startups, however, do grow to become massive corporations, so while the risk is high, the potential for returns if you find the right company is equally enormous (think of companies like Revolut, BrewDog, Peloton, and Oculus VR, who have all crowdfunded in the past).

While the risk is high with crowdfunding, the potential for returns if you find the right company is equally enormous.

How does it work?

1 **Create account**—You create a user account on a platform such as Indiegogo, Seedrs, or Crowdcube (there are many more).

2 **Research**—From there you can browse all the companies that are currently fundraising. Each company will have a profile page with an introductory video explaining who they are, what they do, and why you should invest in them, along with many other documents and information.

3 **Invest**—Most crowdfunding campaigns will be open for just a few weeks, so you have to be pretty quick (this is, of course, no excuse not to do your research before investing).

4 **Remember costs**—Keep in mind that investments inevitably entail costs, so it's important to verify the fees levied by the crowdfunding platform.

How much money do I need to invest?

Depending on the platform and company, you can typically get started with around $20. Some companies will also state a maximum investment amount, to make sure there is room for as many investors as possible. (This amount will vary from company to company.)

How do I get my money back?

Generally speaking, you can get your money back in three ways:

- If another investor wants to buy your shares in the company (some platforms can facilitate this through a so-called "secondary market").
- If the company gets sold to another company.
- If the company goes public and gets listed on a stock exchange.

In most cases you should expect your money to be invested for at least five years.

Crypto Ⓑ

Cryptocurrencies—often abbreviated as crypto—are digital or virtual currencies that don't exist in any physical form, only on a digital network. Many cryptocurrencies use a decentralized technology (often called blockchain) to secure the funds, but also to make it possible to safely transfer these currencies (also called coins or tokens) from one user to the other.

Did you know?

There are thousands of cryptocurrencies, and not all of them are tradeable. The term "crypto" is as broad as "stocks," with each cryptocurrency having a unique purpose. Some coins serve real-world functions, such as being used for payments or network fees, while others lack utility and are used only for price speculation/trading.

Both as a technology and an asset class cryptocurrencies are fast developing. While there are ongoing debates about their value and use, cryptocurrencies are likely to endure in some form. If you are interested in investing we recommend that you dedicate more time to learning and researching before you make any investment decisions.

WHAT YOU NEED TO KNOW

One of the defining characteristics of cryptocurrencies is that they are mostly controlled by the users on the network and not by a government, bank, or a central institution. How exactly the decentralized network and mechanism works depends heavily on the cryptocurrency itself, as there are many ways to make this possible. The most well-known and largest cryptocurrency is Bitcoin, which uses a mechanism called proof-of-work. Without getting too technical, it is basically computers that solve difficult equations, which is considered to be a very safe technology.

A big investing challenge in the crypto world is that it is vastly unregulated. While a company listed on the stock exchange needs to comply with many regulations on marketing and communication regarding what it promises to its customer, many crypto companies have been called out for misleading communication.[13] Even though this is changing now and regulators are picking up on this, being extra careful not to believe promises that sound too good to be true is very important.

The potential impact

Being digital, you might not immediately think cryptocurrency has much environmental impact, but in fact it has a significant carbon footprint.

Environmental impact

Every year it's estimated that Bitcoin mining requires more energy than the total energy consumption of medium-sized countries like Belgium[14], Sweden, or Malaysia[15]. This is because it requires thousands and thousands of high-tech computers to run 24/7. Noting the potentially disastrous consequences of this energy intensive process, New York State is the first to have banned Bitcoin mining.[16]

Even though some argue that the entire traditional banking industry and the printing of cash itself also require a lot of electricity, ultimately there is no way around the fact that Bitcoin has a negative environmental impact.

However, this only holds true for a few cryptocurrencies and mostly only for those that use proof-of-work mechanism. There are many other cryptocurrencies that use different mechanisms and technologies which do not require computers to run 24/7. One prominent alternative mechanism is called proof-of-stake, which is now used by the world's second-largest cryptocurrency, Ethereum. The great thing is that the mechanism needs 99 percent less electricity[17] and is therefore considered much more environmentally friendly, while still being considered very safe.

Why don't all cryptocurrencies use the energy-saving mechanism? Actually, most of them do, but Bitcoin is still by far the biggest digital coin, so the negative environmental impact of crypto as a whole continues to be tremendous.

The heroines of Hera

The political crisis in Afghanistan in 2021 triggered the collapse of the country's economy. However, thanks to the efforts of Fereshteh Forough, an Afghan-based social activist, "Code to Inspire" was set up in Hera in 2016. Over 350 girls learned to code through Forough's academy while it was still possible for women to move freely and engage in education. When the economy and currency took a nose dive in 2021, the girls who had learned to code managed to maintain the crypto wallets they had developed during their coding course. This meant that family and other donors could send crypto to them when many other methods of sending money were blocked due to international sanctions.[19] This often meant these girls were the sole earners in the household and could even fund their family's escape from the country as the situation deteriorated. It goes to show that crypto can be an important means of getting funds and investment to people in countries who most need it when all traditional avenues are blocked.

Social impact

One characteristic of crypto that many regard as a social advantage is that banks and governments cannot control your money. This is because they have no access to, for example, your Bitcoins, which are on the blockchain. There are billions of people who do not have access to bank accounts and the traditional finance system, which means that cryptocurrencies help to level out the playing field and enable more people to participate in the financial markets.

But all this freedom has downsides. First of all, if you have your Bitcoins on the blockchain, only you can access them. So if you lose your access code (this is called a "private key"), no one on this planet can help you to get your money back. You are fully responsible for your own funds. Such a thing could never happen on the stock market because all your investments are registered to your personal identification number, so it's impossible to "lose" them. And even when you lose your online banking password, you can call your bank to restore it. You being the only person who has access also means that no government or bank can freeze your account or stop you accessing your funds. That might sound like a very unlikely scenario, but in some cases, and especially for people who live under corrupt governments, this can be hugely beneficial. (See the box

opposite for the story of 350 girls in Afghanistan who would have lost everything if it wasn't for cryptocurrencies.)

But there are also critics of the fact that no government or bank can interfere with the transfer of funds. They argue that crypto networks can easily be used for ill-intended purposes, such as funding criminals or bypassing international sanctions. While criminals can (and do) use cryptocurrencies, too, the use of crypto for illicit activities seems to comprise only a small part of the overall cryptocurrency economy, and it appears to be much smaller than the amount of illicit funds involved in traditional finance.[18] However, it is not possible to decide not to buy Bitcoins from a person who is involved in money laundering or a cocaine dealer.

The negative environmental impact of crypto continues to be tremendous.

HOW CAN I GET INVOLVED— AND SHOULD I?

As tends to be the case in this book, the answer depends on you and your values. While the environmental impact is heavily dependent on the specific cryptocurrency and therefore can be mitigated, for the societal impact, it comes down to one question: do you believe decentralized networks are good or bad for society?

How does it work?

1 **Research**—Since crypto is significantly more complicated than the other asset classes we have introduced you to, we encourage you to learn more about the technology before buying (such as who is behind it, how the technology behind it actually works, and, of course, whether it uses the power-hungry proof-of-work mechanism).

2 **Create a profile**—To buy cryptocurrencies you create a profile on a crypto exchange, which is a broker specifically for cryptocurrencies. Examples of such exchanges are Kraken, Binance, and Coinbase, which are all currently among the biggest in the world. Had this book been written one year previously, we would likely have included the now-bankrupt broker FTX (see page 110), which emphasizes the importance of point 4, below.

3 **Invest**—Once you have access to an exchange, the process of buying and selling crypto is essentially the same as that for buying and selling stocks in

terms of buy and sell buttons and all other options that you also know from a stockbroker.

4 **Move to wallet**—The final step is slightly technical, but very important. Unlike with stocks, you need to actually move your cryptocurrency from the exchange to your own wallet, so that if anything happens to the exchange your money is safe. To withdraw your coins you need a wallet on the respective blockchain. Some of the safest wallets are very similar to a USB stick and are called hardware wallets (popular ones are Trezor or Ledger, which can be bought for around $100). Make sure you know how to access your wallet, while at the same time don't tell anyone your access codes and try to prevent others finding it out—don't write it down!

How much money do I need?

Technically you can start by investing less than $100, but similar to investing in stocks, crypto exchanges charge you a fee every time you either buy or sell coins. Therefore, we recommend that you invest at least $300 per trade, so that the fees don't eat up too much of your potential returns. And even though you can buy coins and just leave them on the exchange account, it is worth buying a hardware wallet to be safe.

At the time of writing, one Bitcoin costs around $25,000—but don't worry, you can often buy fractions of a coin for significantly smaller amounts.

How do I get my money back?

Similar to buying stocks and funds, you can earn money on crypto in two primary ways:

- By selling your coins at a higher price than you paid.
- By getting the equivalent of dividends, which are called staking rewards. Here, you often need to lock your coins and "put them to work" on the blockchain or network. As a reward you will receive a small percentage of the transaction fee on an ongoing basis.

The crypto market is very liquid, meaning there are many buyers and sellers at all times, so it's both easy and fast to get your money back.

Chaos on the crypto exchange

In 2022 one of the world's largest crypto exchanges, FTX, went bankrupt within days. Pretty much all the money and cryptocurrencies from customers that were on that exchange, worth billions and billions, were lost.[20] So what happened?

In November 2022 news about many illicit and possibly criminal activities of FTX[21] triggered numerous big investors to withdraw money from FTX. Immediately people stormed the website to withdraw their money as well, only to see an error message stating that FTX had stopped withdrawals—customers couldn't access their money. This is what's called a bank run. All customers want the money back that they deposited but the bank (in this case FTX) doesn't actually have it anymore. A few days later, FTX filed for bankruptcy, losing more than $8 billion of customers' money.[22]

At the time of writing, a lot of court rulings are still outstanding, and special attention is put on former CEO Sam Bankman-Fried. But as in most bankruptcy cases, the chance of customers who had their money in accounts owned by FTX getting their money back is slim. The current CEO of FTX is John J. Ray III, who specializes in recovering funds from failed corporations. Speaking of the previous management, Ray stated: "Never in my career have I seen such a complete failure of corporate controls and such a complete absence of trustworthy financial information as occurred here." He added that "this situation is unprecedented."[23]

Angel *investing*

An angel investor is someone who invests their money into a small, privately owned business, usually in exchange for some ownership of the company.[24] It is a way of getting businesses that are changing the world the attention they deserve.

WHAT YOU NEED TO KNOW

Most angels invest in a startup early in the company's lifetime and usually take a slightly more hands-on approach compared to larger investors, who may join at a later stage. They often have specific in-depth knowledge of the field and industry and therefore offer both funding and guidance in exchange for the ownership that they gain in the company. They can also choose whether to give money once, multiple times, as a lump sum, or in multiple small pots, which will eventually affect their returns and how they exit the investment.

Did you know?

The phrase angel investing first started in Broadway theaters, when production teams, actors, and others in the arts would go to wealthy individuals to get their play on the stage.[25]

Did you know?

Between 2010 and 2019 there were an estimated 39,963 angel deals made globally and it's likely that the real figures are larger, given the private nature of angel investments. The US dominates these deals with 95% being in the United States, followed by Europe, of which the UK and France take the top spots regionally.[28]

In the US the average angel investing check is around $25,000 and comes directly from the pockets of private investors.[26] As it's all about personal relationships, networking, and rubbing shoulders with those who have money in their pockets, female entrepreneurs are hugely under-represented among the founders who receive funding from angel investing. Stats show that startups with at least one female founder received 17% of angel funding in 2021, while female-only founder teams received just 2% of that figure.[27] Canada and Germany raise the flag for having the worst gender-funding gaps across the largest 10 angel-investing countries.

Proportion of Total National Angel Capital Received by Gender[29]

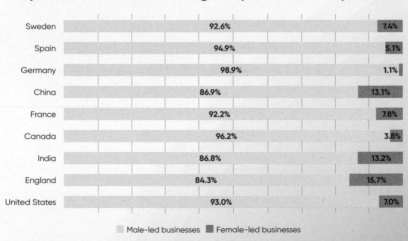

Country	Male-led businesses	Female-led businesses
Sweden	92.6%	7.4%
Spain	94.9%	5.1%
Germany	98.9%	1.1%
China	86.9%	13.1%
France	92.2%	7.8%
Canada	96.2%	3.8%
India	86.8%	13.2%
England	84.3%	15.7%
United States	93.0%	7.0%

■ Male-led businesses ■ Female-led businesses

It's also worth noting that these figures are for female-led businesses. Not even majority or solely women, just female-led, with men on the founding team, too. Obviously, there's some serious work to do.

The potential impact

Similar to crowdfunding, the potential impact of angel investing is great, but it will naturally depend heavily on the company you invest in. That said, given the hands-on approach of most angel investments, it is one of the most powerful ways by which you as an individual can help a company to get off the ground. At Female Invest, we have benefited tremendously from the support, guidance, and network that was given to us by the angels that invested in us in the early days of our journey. They played a crucial role in helping us get started and the impact they have had on our company from the very beginning is undeniable. In fact, so much so that we have dedicated this book to two of our angel investors.

Again, we strongly encourage anyone who has the means to angel invest to prioritize all the great ventures that are founded by women and minorities, most of which are underfunded and will never get the chance to hit the ground running without external capital and support.

Did you know?

Angel investing involves bigger investments from a smaller number of people, whereas crowdfunding involves smaller investments from a larger number of people.

HOW CAN I GET INVOLVED— AND SHOULD I?

It's a bit of a misperception that angel investing is an arena exclusively for billionaires. Many angels are in fact successful investors, lawyers, doctors, entrepreneurs, or those who have been lucky to inherit larger sums of money.[30] However, there is no way around it—in order to be an angel investor, you do need to be relatively well off and ready to invest tens of thousands of dollars into one company, while also being fully prepared that there is a high risk of losing it all.

Anyone who is in a financial situation that enables them to participate in angel investing can do so relatively easily. The biggest issue you will encounter is most likely finding a company that resonates with you and that you believe has what it takes to go the distance. Therefore, networking and getting involved in the startup scene in your local community will be critical to your success as an angel investor.

How does it work?

1 **Identify startups**—The more startups you know, the higher the chance of finding a potential future unicorn (see opposite). A great way to meet founders is to go to startup conferences, networking events, and even reach out through LinkedIn. When it comes to angel investing, your network is your net worth.

2 **Research the company**—Conducting thorough research on a company is vital for making informed investment decisions. Start by analyzing the business model, financials, management team, market position, customer feedback, and any potential legal challenges (more details on how to do this are covered in Chapter 7). It is customary to simply request this information from the company. As with all investments, comprehensive understanding will help you to identify promising opportunities and mitigate any risks.

3 **Agree on terms**—Once you have found a company that you want to invest in (and who wants to accept your money), then you have to agree the terms of the transaction. For

very young companies this will typically be a relatively easy, back-of-the-napkin kind of agreement. One of the most important things to agree on is the valuation of the company, which will dictate the price of the shares you buy.

4 **Do the paperwork**—Although it is likely to be very casual, it is a good idea to get a lawyer involved who can draft a shareholders' agreement (if one doesn't already exist), so that each party knows exactly what their rights are. The lawyer will also help with the contracts and ensure that the new ownership is reported to the authorities and the money is transferred safely from you to the startup.

5 **Align expectations**—It is a good idea to align expectations with the management/founding team of the startup with regards to how active you will be and how many hours (if any) you plan on working with the company.

Did you know?

The word "unicorn" is used to describe a startup with a value of over $1 billion. This term was invented by the venture capitalist Aileen Lee in 2013. Since then, it has become well-known startup lingo used around the world.

How much money do I need?

There is no strict minimum investment amount, this will depend on what you agree with the startup. However, research shows that an average check size for an angel investment is between $15,000 and $250,000.[31, 32] If you have the capital (and network) for it, it's great to spread your risk by investing in several companies. Many angel investors end up having a whole portfolio of startup investments.

How do I get my money back?

There are a few ways you can do this:

- If the company performs incredibly well and decides to pay out dividends to its shareholders (this is very rare for startups, as they typically have several years of being far from profitable).
- If a larger institutional investor (typically a venture capital fund) wants to invest, then they may sometimes want to buy out older investors.
- If the company gets acquired by another company, who buys all the shares from the various investors.
- If the company goes public (IPO) and lists on a stock exchange.

It takes many years to build a great company, so you should expect your money to be invested for at least five to seven years. Although the risk is high, research has shown that 33% of angel investments pay back between one and five times the invested amount.[33]

If your personal finances aren't quite geared for writing big checks for single companies, but you like the idea of helping to give young businesses a chance, remember that crowdfunding has many of the same benefits, albeit on a smaller scale (see pages 96–103).

When it comes to angel investing, your network is your net worth.

Property

Long seen as a cornerstone of embracing "adult life," home ownership is something that we dream of, but sadly the dream feels increasingly out of reach for many millennials. In the US, data shows that only 39% of millennials owned homes in 2015 compared to 47.5% for that same age group in 2007.[34] This also explains why the number of first-time buyers is hovering near 30-year lows in most western countries.

First-time home-buyers—many of them millennials—find themselves in a perfect storm, according to economist Lawrence Yun of the National Association of REALTORS®. Rents are rising faster than wages, making it hard for renters to save for a downpayment or get an attractive loan.[35, 36]

A brief history of women and property

In ancient Egypt, women had full rights to buy, hold, and sell their own property, but these rights were removed, and it took nearly 2,000 years for women across the world to regain or gain them. While certain societies maintained women's property rights even after marriage, many others revoked these privileges once women wed. Mississippi, in 1839, became the first US state to permit women to own property in their own names, yet they were still subject to restrictions, like needing their husband's permission to open a bank account. In Ireland, it wasn't until 1976 that women were finally allowed to own a house outright. In Africa, women still rarely own the rights to their property, leaving them in a precarious position should they ever lose their husband.[37]

Sadly (but probably unsurprising at this point), the situation is worse for women. A report by the Women's Budget Group in 2019 found women in the UK need nearly 12 times their annual salary to buy a property, whereas men only need around eight times as much.[38] There is little hope that this statistic is different anywhere else in the world.

Facts like these can be incredibly disheartening and frustrating, but did you know that there are actually several ways in which you can invest in the housing market for a fraction of the money required to buy a full property? In the following pages we will walk you through the most common options for getting your foot on the property ladder in, of course, the most sustainable way possible.

More specifically, that means we will deep dive into the following ways by which you can invest in property:

1   Buying and living in your own property.
2   Buy to rent.
3   Real Estate Investment Trust (REIT).
4   Pooled/joint property investment.

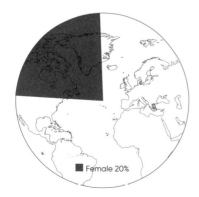

Female 20%

Globally, women only own 20% of the world's land.[39]

1. Buying and living in *your* own property

Many of us dream about having the freedom and excitement of owning our own home—and with good reason. But buying property is most likely one of the biggest financial decisions you will ever make, so it's important to think through the pros and cons carefully.

Did you know?

Despite rising costs of living, property investing is popular among millennials. In the US, 50% of millennial investors choose to invest in property. This may sound like a high number and it's a drop from the previous generation, but it's not as significant a drop as you might think—when Gen X was the same age as millennials today, their homeownership rate was 58%.[40]

WHAT YOU NEED TO KNOW

On the positive side, owning and living in your own property gives you (almost) full control over your space. This gives you a lot of creative freedom and means you can design a home that is perfect for you (and your family). At the same time you never have to worry about rising rental prices again—in fact, you will benefit if the housing market sees an upturn, because the resale price of your property will likely follow suit.

The biggest downside to owning property is very simple: the capital requirement—often in the form of a substantial down payment. But owning property also comes with a lot of financial responsibility, such as general maintenance and fixing broken parts. Let's say, for example, the heating system in your own house breaks down—you have to

pay for that repair yourself and no one will compensate you.

Another key consideration is the lack of flexibility that comes with property ownership. Maybe your family grows and you need to move for a new job opportunity, or you want to be closer to an aging parent? While some real estate markets are very liquid, meaning it's relatively easy and fast to sell your property, this is not always the case and sometimes it can take months or even years to sell a house, not to mention the financial considerations of selling costs and taxes due. Therefore, how long you plan on staying in your place is an important factor to consider before buying.

The potential impact
When buying property the potential for impact investment is relatively limited. However, choosing a more sustainable option that has been designed, built, or even perhaps altered to function in a more environmentally sound way is a good step.

HOW CAN I GET INVOLVED— AND SHOULD I?

In short, if you can afford it, yes.

How does it work?

1 Assuming you don't have the money to pay the full price of a property, the first step is to talk to your bank to understand how much you might be able to borrow. The bank probably won't be able to give you final approvals until you have an actual property in mind, but it's great to understand what your options and limitations are before you go looking for property and set your heart on something you can't afford.

2 With this information, it's time to make a budget. There are a lot of variables to play around with, so it's a good idea to note down all the possible costs, so you have a full overview (including a loan, taxes, construction/ renovation fees, Realtor commission, etc.).

Have you heard of the "Starbucks effect on property"?

In their book *Zillow Talk: The New Rules of Real Estate,* chief executive Spencer Rascoff and chief economist Stan Humphries discuss the impact that the opening of a Starbucks store can have on local property values and the surrounding neighborhood. When a Starbucks store opens in an area, it is often seen as a signal of local improvement and increased economic activity.

In the book, the authors "found that homes within a quarter-mile of a Starbucks rose in value an average of 96 percent between 1997 and 2014, compared with 65 percent for all US homes."

While it might be interesting to monitor new store openings to assess the potential of a given area, the "Starbucks effect" is not a guarantee, and various other factors, such as the overall economic climate and the specific dynamics of the local property market, always play a role in determining property values.

3 Start looking for properties that live up to your criteria. A lot of this can be done online via real estate websites. Once you find a great place and make an offer, it's time to talk to the bank again to get it approved.

4 Take the offer from your bank and speak with other banks to see if you can get a better deal. Small changes in interest rate will have a tremendous impact on how good the investment will be, so make sure that you don't accept the first offer—the banks can do better!

5 Once you have the best offer in your hand, you are all set to buy the property.

While the process does not vary much from country to country, it's important that you understand all the different processes and possible pitfalls involved in purchasing property (such as taxes and legal fees).

How much money do I need?
The required down payment differs from country to country, but usually it is between 5 and 20% of the purchase price. So all things considered, if you were to buy an condominium for $200,000 you would likely need between $10,000 and $40,000 as a deposit.

How do I get my money back?
Quite simply by selling the house at a higher price than you paid. Indirectly, even without selling you get money back, as you are most likely not paying rent anymore, which is often more expensive than mortgage repayments. So even if you never sell your house, it might still be a great long-term investment.

Unfortunately, there is no guarantee the housing market will continue to climb or that any money you put into improvements will be reflected in the price at which you sell the property. So make sure to strike a balance between creating your unique dream house and being able to attract buyers down the line. Always remember, too, that there are three elements that matter the most in setting the price of a property: location, location, and location.

2. Buying *to rent*

While the process of purchasing property for the purpose of renting it out is almost identical to buying a home to live in, the planning process, the specifications of the house and area, and what comes after differs.

What is the ideal rental income?

When investing in rental properties, it's a good idea to calculate the Price-to-Rent ratio. This indicates the number of years required to accumulate enough rent to cover the property's purchase price. To calculate the ratio, simply divide the buying price by the annual rent. For example, if an condo costs $240,000 and yields $12,000 in annual rent, the Price-to-Rent ratio is 20, meaning it would take 20 years to break even on the property's purchase price.

A lower Price-to-Rent ratio (or higher Annual Rent Yield percentage) makes renting out the property more attractive. While the definition of a "good" ratio varies based on location, ratios below 15 are generally considered decent investment opportunities. However, a ratio of 20 (like the example provided) can still be profitable if the property's value appreciates significantly, resulting in a favorable return upon selling. The ratio can fluctuate widely depending on the city; for instance, expensive cities like San Francisco, London, or Hong Kong often have ratios above 20, while economically challenged areas like Detroit may have ratios below 5.

To determine the Price-to-Rent ratio for your specific city, visit a prominent real estate website in your area and conduct searches for both buying and renting. Select a few comparable properties and make a few hypothetical calculations.

WHAT YOU NEED TO KNOW

The best way to think about buying property to rent out (buy to rent) is to treat it as a small company. You have investment costs, ongoing expenses (such as taxes, fees, and, of course, interest payments), and revenue in the form of rental income. So before buying a property, you will have to sit down and calculate the business case for your property— what is the sum of all the costs and how much do you expect to earn?

While you will encounter the same unexpected costs that you do when living in your own property (for example, a water leak, or the fridge breaks down and you need to replace it) there is also an element of revenue uncertainty. You need to expect months without rent. That can be due to a tenant moving out and you struggling to find a replacement or, even worse, getting a bad tenant who for some reason doesn't pay their rent on time. Unfortunately your bank won't care and will still expect your monthly mortgage payment.

The potential impact

Obviously you have the freedom to make your rental property as sustainable as you like, but there are also a few options to improve the ethics and social impact.

Unique benefits when investing in property

1. Invest in property to protect against inflation: During periods of high inflation, many asset classes struggle while real estate flourishes. The reason for this is that as inflation rates rise, the value of your property also rises, along with any rental income you might generate. So, during periods of inflation, landlords have the opportunity to create greater profits.

2. Property investment can bring tax benefits: Most countries offer plentiful tax benefits when you invest in real estate. For example, you might be allowed to deduct various expenses such as appreciation, mortgage interest, maintenance costs, and more. That said, it's essential that you discuss your financial affairs with a tax specialist or financial advisor while filing taxes to make sure you qualify for certain tax benefits.

Did you know?

The world of buy-to-rent investing has traditionally been dominated by men. However, current figures reveal that women now make up 48% of the 2.6 million buy-to-rent investors in the UK.[41]

48%

2.6 million buy-to-rent UK investors

Social impact

Some people question the social ethics behind renting out properties, arguing that it contributes to the housing crisis that is sweeping through many countries, enabling landlords to be greedy and trapping those who can't afford to buy into a long-term cycle of renting. The ethics of renting is one of those sustainable investing dilemmas that we could debate for much longer than the length of this book, but the good thing is that you have an active choice.

First of all, you can choose to keep your rent at fair market value by not overcharging. As a landlord you also have the opportunity to take an active stance against racial discrimination, which is a huge problem in many countries. One study in the US found that applicants with an African American or Hispanic/Latinx-sounding name were more than 40% less likely to receive answers from rental listings than those with presumably "white"-sounding names.[42]

Another option is to invest in social housing, where you're providing a roof over the head of someone who may have otherwise been homeless, or who is between accommodations.[43] With 58% of social housing occupants in the UK being women, the gender imbalances in property is undeniable.[44] By offering affordable housing to these women, or other vulnerable groups, you can help break negative cycles of homelessness and also earn a steady rate of return in the form of rental income. Many countries offer special programs where you can register your house to be recognized as a social house, which in some instances will also qualify you for additional subsidies from the government.

HOW CAN I GET INVOLVED— AND SHOULD I?

Once you have decided to go ahead and have found a property where you believe the business case is strong, it is up to you to make it a great impact investment that positively contributes to society.

How does it work?

1   A good starting point is to compare the prices for the properties for sale with the rental cost of similar properties. A rule of thumb is that to invest in a property, you should get at least 4–5% return on the purchase price per annum. If a 540-square-foot condominium in your city costs $200,000 to buy and you can rent it out for $1,000 a month (which is $12,000 a year), this means that your return on investment is $12,000/$200.000 = 6%. Of course this is just a broad

indication, but the higher that percentage is, the better, and therefore the better your investment.

2   Make a business case. With the possible return in mind, map out all the likely costs and also consider the risk and impact on your finances of not getting rent for a month or even longer.

3   Once you have done the research, it's time to buy a property. Some banks might offer different loans if you don't live in the apartment yourself, and sometimes different taxes apply, but other than that, the process is the same as above.

How much money do I need?
To no surprise, this is similar to buying a house and living in it. So assume 5–20% of the purchase price.

How do I get my money back?
You get your money back continuously through the rental income you receive while you are paying off your mortgage, and more when it is paid off.

3. Real Estate Investment Trusts (*REIT*)

REITs (Real Estate Investment Trusts) are a type of fund that brings investors together to buy multiple properties, much like other funds that invest into stocks.

WHAT YOU NEED TO KNOW

The group of properties that is bought by the fund usually follows an overarching theme. The unique element of REITs is that you often get paid the equivalent of the rent that these incomes generate minus a fee, which is potentially an excellent source of passive income. REITs are typically traded just like stocks and ETFs on exchanges via a broker. This liquidity makes it easier to buy or sell shares as needed.

Professional management
REITs are managed by experienced professionals who handle property acquisitions, management, and operations. Investors can benefit from the expertise of these professionals without getting involved in day-to-day management.

REITs often focus on specific real estate sectors, allowing investors to target areas they believe will perform well without having to manage individual properties themselves.

The value of REITs can be influenced by factors such as interest rates, economic conditions, and the real estate market. It's essential to research and assess the specific REIT's track record, portfolio, and financial health before making an investment decision.

The potential for impact

Generally speaking, the impact created through REITs is less transparent, but there are a few ways to optimize the ethics.

Social and environmental impact

There are ways for you to directly invest in social housing, but there are also funds that help with the issue of affordability, known as "social housing REITs." These have several social housing properties spread across different locations (sometimes even across several countries), which is a great way to diversify and minimize your risk. Some funds have launched sustainable REITs, which focus on things such as construction of net-zero properties or acquiring high energy efficiency credentials.

The value of REITs can be influenced by many factors, so always research and assess the specific REIT's track record before making an investment decision.

HOW CAN I GET INVOLVED— AND SHOULD I?

Getting into REITs is easy. They are widely available and the minimum capital requirements are typically very low. You can almost consider REITs an alternative to stocks or an ETF. Transparency in this area is not always great and in some countries there are certain tax implications, so it's critical that you do your own research and read the fine print prior to committing any capital.

How does it work?

1 Look for a broker in your country that offers REITs.

2 Create a user profile and start researching—if you know you want REITs that cover a particular geographical area, start looking for those.

3 Although it's usually very similar to stocks, the tax implications of REITs differ from country to country, so make sure you know how your potential returns will be taxed.

4 Buy and sell REITs in the same way that you buy and sell stocks.

How do I get my money back?
REITs are very similar to funds, so there are two ways to get your money back:

- Sell them at a higher price than you paid.
- Earn dividends in the form of rental income if the properties in the fund are rented out.

Did you know?

REITs are volatile like stocks, but they are not closely correlated to the performance of the stock market. You can see this because they move up or down at different times and in different magnitudes than stocks. This makes them a good choice for portfolio diversification.

4. Pooled/joined *property investments*

Pooling money to buy property is another good investment option, which also requires significantly less capital. While this is in theory possible to do with friends and family (always be careful when mixing money with friendships), new platforms have recently emerged that enable strangers to contribute to a purchase for this exact purpose.

WHAT YOU NEED TO KNOW

The concept is very similar to crowdfunding, where you use a third-party platform to buy a share in a property. There are many new players in this market, so it's important that you look into the company behind the platform to ensure they are legitimate and worthy of your investment.

The potential impact
Unlike REITs, you can typically choose the specific properties you want to invest in, which means you have full transparency.

Social and environmental impact
You will know if your money is going toward a factory that produces chemicals or a new apartment building that is built using best-in-class sustainability measures. Personally, though, you have very little influence—if any—on who the tenant will be, if the owners discriminate against marginalized groups, or if they actually want to create a positive living environment.

HOW CAN I GET INVOLVED— AND SHOULD I?

These types of investments can be a great way to diversify your portfolio, since you can invest in property in different countries, or in industrial property or infrastructure, which you otherwise wouldn't have access to.

How does it work?
Here are two approaches. The first is similar to crowdfunding:

1 Find platforms that facilitate property investment (there are dozens of crowdfunding platforms, depending on the country you live in).

2 Sign up to a platform you trust, then start browsing the available properties and invest.

How much money do I need?
This depends on whether you use a crowdfunding platform to buy the property or if you pool your money with friends and family.

If you invest via a crowdfunding platform, then you get a share of a certain property for as little as $20 or $100, depending on which platform you use. You can increase this amount as much as you like to get a bigger piece of the cake. This is great, because you don't have to invest in lawyers or worry about any contracts, loans, or regulation. The platform will handle everything.

If you are investing with friends and family, this will depend on how many of you are partaking in the investment. If there are 10 of you, simply divide the price of the property by 10 to calculate what the down payment is for each of you.

How do I get my money back?
You can get your money back in a few different ways:

- If there is any rental income this will be paid out continuously between the owners of the property based on how large your shareholding is.

- If the building gets sold by the crowdfunding platform, the profits plus any rental income are divided among the owners based on how large your shareholding is. Keep in mind that the platform also has to earn money, so their fees will be charged before anything else is paid out.

- Some crowdfunding platforms have a secondaries market where shares of certain properties can be traded among investors (without the property itself being sold).

INVESTMENT OPPORTUNITIES AT A GLANCE

INVESTMENT CLASS	STOCKS	BONDS	EFTS
What is it?	Buying a small part of a company	Giving a loan, e.g. to the government or a large company	A bundle of assets following a theme (e.g. an industry)
What should you consider?	Individual stocks can be hard to pick. They have higher risk and potential return than, say, bonds	High—when investing in green bonds, on the primary market, as they directly fund projects with clear environmental benefits	An easy way to diversify risk
What's the potential impact?	High—when many investors start setting demands, companies have to listen	High—when investing in green bonds, as they directly fund projects with clear environmental benefits	This depends on the theme of the ETF. You can invest in anything from "fossil fuels" to "green energy"

PROPERTY	CROWD INVESTING	CRYPTO	ANGEL INVESTING
Owning and renting out property	Investing small amounts of money in startups along with a large number of other investors	Owning digital assets such as Bitcoin	Investing larger amounts directly into a startup
A lot of responsibility, but big potential	High-risk and very long term, but a chance to diversify	Very risky and difficult to truly assess the value	Risky and large commitment, but high potential returns
Low—Aside from using sustainable materials and being a fair landlord, impact is limited	High—if you support companies with a positive impact or founders from diverse backgrounds	Low—you likely don't have a positive impact simply by buying a cryptocurrency	High—if you support companies with a positive impact or founders from diverse backgrounds

Key takeaways

The world of investing is much bigger than stocks, funds, and bonds. Learning about alternative investments is a powerful tool to optimize your portfolio and have an even bigger impact. This chapter has covered the following types of alternative investments:

- **Crowdfunding:** Investing directly in companies that are not listed on the stock exchange alongside many other investors. Typically, crowdfunding involves smaller investments from a large number of people.
- **Cryptocurrencies:** Digital currencies that don't exist in any physical form and are controlled by the users on the network rather than governments and financial institutions (well-known examples include Bitcoin and Ethereum).

- **Angel investing:** Investing your personal funds in startups in exchange for equity ownership and the potential for financial returns. Angel investing involves bigger investments from a smaller number of people, whereas crowdfunding involves smaller investments from a large number of people.
- **Property:** Property investing refers to buying and owning real estate. If you don't want to buy an entire property, there are multiple alternatives that often don't require a lot of money. Examples include REITs and joined property investments.

Strategies for impact investing

What is an investment strategy?

Now that you know what you can invest in, it's time to make an investment strategy. A strategy is what dictates how you assemble your portfolio—the assets you choose to invest in —and the behaviors that guide those decisions.

As you read through this chapter, please remember: stepping into your financial power is an iterative process rather than a fixed result, and so is making the perfect investment strategy. However, with the right strategy, your money becomes a weapon.

Are you ready to pull the trigger?

Remember, it's not just about changing your own financial future; this is about changing the future for generations to come.

THREE APPROACHES FOR IMPACT INVESTING

Risk and diversification

Diversification is key to long-term success when investing. Why? Because when picking individual investments, there are no guarantees on how they will perform. Unforeseen events could happen or the market conditions could change. Therefore, it's important to not put all of your eggs in one basket and invest in many different assets across industries and continents. However, if you only buy impact investments (as in the "maximum impact" strategy), it will be very difficult to diversify. As a result, you take on a much higher risk with a large potential for a lower return. To mitigate this, you may want to avoid strategy 3 and consider including investments that don't live up to all of your impact demands.

Hopefully you're fully on board with thinking about what sustainability means to you and the causes you're eager to help with your investing.

How much you include sustainability in your investing can be broken down into three strategies, which can be translated into strengths of sustainability. We like to think of them as starting with a very light dusting of green on a blank canvas, all the way through to the strongest, boldest green color you can imagine covering the entire picture.

1 Do no harm

As the name suggests, this strategy implies removing all investments that can objectively be classified as "harmful" and therefore do no harm. The companies you invest in don't necessarily have to be front runners in saving the world, but they also can't harm it. The easiest way to do this is by actively excluding companies and industries that you believe cause harm to the planet or its people.

You can apply this strategy to most forms of investing. The way that it's measured and gauged might be slightly different, but the key focus of this investing strategy is that there is no negativity. There is nothing doing any harm in the portfolio.

Balanced approach, please

With the previous strategy of excluding harmful investments, you can still leave room for investments that aren't particularly impactful, as long as they do not harm.

Through the implementation of this strategy, you not only avoid detrimental enterprises, but actively opt for investments that directly contribute to a positive impact. Concurrently, you create space for additional investments that might lack a clear positive societal influence, yet avoid causing harm. A classic and often used example of this is allocating the bulk of your portfolio to prominent funds, while complementing it with a selection of individual stocks that strongly prioritize ESG considerations.

Maximum impact

This strategy represents the most robust form of impact investing, verging on the extreme, as it exclusively targets companies actively engaged in improving the world. According to the World Bank Group, impact investing under this strategy involves "actively contributing to measure social and environmental impact alongside financial returns."[1] It's not just about avoiding harm or including a few sustainable choices within the overall investment portfolio. Rather, it focuses exclusively on the positive impact.

Although the S&P Global discovered that many ESG funds outperformed the overall market benchmark during the pandemic, it's important to note that impact investing in its most extreme form may not yield comparable returns to the other outlined strategies.[2] The rationale behind this is that an extreme emphasis on impact could lead to the exclusion of numerous diversification opportunities, thereby heightening risk and reducing the likelihood of achieving the average market return. However, if you are willing to trade off some returns in favor of impact, then this approach could be suitable for you.

FIVE STEPS TO BUILDING AN IMPACT PORTFOLIO

 Decide what your goals are

Before making any investment, it's important to know what your life goals are, as these will heavily influence how much risk you should be taking and how long you should aim to have your money invested. For example, if you're a student or newly graduated, most people's goals are to minimize or pay off their student debt. If you have been working full-time for some years, your goal might be to get on the property ladder. If you're older and later in life, goals typically revolve around saving enough to sustain your lifestyle into retirement.

No matter what your goal is, the key is to note how much money is required and how many years you have to achieve it. Generally speaking, the more years you can afford to leave your money invested, the more risk you can afford to take. This is great because risk and reward go hand in hand, meaning the higher the risk, the higher the chance for greater returns.

2 Decide which values are most important to you

As discussed in Chapter 3, defining which values matter most to you (in a business context) is important, so you know where to place your focus. Many values related to ESG might overlap. For example, social criteria may overlap with environmental criteria and governance when companies seek to comply with environmental laws and broader concerns about sustainability.[3] But it is still a good idea to know which matters the most to you. Below is a list for inspiration:

- Low carbon emissions
- Corporate governance
- Data privacy and security
- Environmental operations
- Environmental supply chain
- Human capital
- Public policy

3 Diversify, diversify, diversify

No matter how many years you have to achieve your goals, diversifying your portfolio is a must.

More diversifying = less risk.

Let's say you only invest in companies that produce wind energy; if a new regulation means it suddenly becomes much harder for these companies to develop wind farms, chances are the stock prices for the entire industry will drop, and all your investments will

More diversification = less risk

follow suit. If only 10 percent of your portfolio was invested in wind energy, then naturally only 10 percent of your portfolio would be affected. That's why it's crucial to invest across different asset classes, different regions, and different industries. As a rule of thumb, the more diverse your portfolio, the less risk you accrue.

 Define your target allocation

Asset allocation is the composition of your portfolio across the different asset types we discussed in the last chapter. For most people the vast majority will consist of stocks, funds, and bonds, but remember, the potential for impact is much bigger in some of the alternative asset classes, such as crowdfunding or angel investing, so by allocating even a small portion of your portfolio toward alternatives, you can have greater impact. The composition heavily influences the amount of risk you're taking on, so it's important to think this through carefully before you invest.[4]

 Do your homework

We will talk about how you research a company's performance and ethics later on, but we just want to emphasize here that you should never make any investments without doing thorough due diligence first.

THE BOTTOM LINE TO IMPACT STRATEGIES

Most things are simpler in life when there's a plan of action, and investing is no exception. Investing in a way that makes the world a better place is something that the vast majority of us strive for—after all, you've picked up this book so it's likely you'll want to make something better, even if it's a small part of society.

Sustainable investing is fantastic, especially if it really does take steps toward changing the world. Don't forget, simply depriving companies that aren't behaving sustainably also has an impact. Be it a drop in the ocean, every little action has wider repercussions.

Defining which values matter most to you is important, so you know where to place your focus.

Researching investment opportunities

Before investing it's absolutely crucial that you do your own research. But what information should you be searching for, and once you find it, how do you analyze it? We get that this part of the process can feel daunting and completely overwhelming, but don't worry, we've got you covered.

Before we get our hands dirty (figuratively speaking, of course) let's first define the key term of this section: "due diligence." Though it sounds technical, due diligence simply refers to diligently researching something.

Don't be like Elon...

If a large company wants to buy another large company, the process will begin with the potential buyer requesting all kinds of information that can be used to make a final investment decision. You might remember that in 2022, billionaire Elon Musk publicly announced and began his acquisition of Twitter. Shortly after the announcement he got cold feet and decided not to go through with the takeover, as the due diligence revealed things he did not like. As the acquisition was already set in motion, Elon was unable to pull out and consequently opted to sue the company. In the end Elon Musk bought Twitter for roughly $44 billion. You might be thinking: "Wait a minute, why are you telling me this story about Elon Musk and why did he progress the investment before doing his due diligence?" The short answer is: Don't be like Elon (at least, not in this case). Always do your due diligence prior to making any investment!

Although we have covered many asset classes throughout the book, the rest of this chapter will focus on how to assess individual companies, because this is the most relevant and often the hardest task. We will first talk about analyzing the health of a company in a traditional business context—for example, is it good at making money and is that likely to continue in the future? Secondly, we will move on to addressing how you can assess the ethics and the ESG factors of a company.

So how is due diligence done as a private investor? Obviously large corporations won't be sending you files and documents for you to review just because you are considering buying some of their shares. However, all publicly traded companies are obligated to disclose relevant information publicly. This covers everything from financial statements, where you can uncover how the company is performing, to strategy documents and impact reports—and all of this can be found online. Generally speaking, the larger the company and the greater the public exposure, the easier the information will be to find. That also means that if you're considering investing in a small company through crowdfunding or angel investing, thorough due diligence will typically be much harder.

BASIC INVESTMENT DUE DILIGENCE

The basic part of a due diligence can be broken down into a few steps. Keep in mind that there is no right or wrong way to research a company. The most important thing is that you understand what you're investing in and that you feel good about your decision. Once you feel satisfied with your understanding of how the company operates today and what it has in store for the future, then you are technically ready to press "buy."

1 Plan your approach

Stock research is as simple as gathering the right materials from the right websites, looking at some key numbers (quantitative research), asking some important questions (qualitative research) and looking at how a company compares to its industry peers—as well as how it compares to itself in the past. You can keep it very high-level or go as deep as you'd like. It's truly a matter of personal preference and how much information you need to feel confident making investment decisions.

- A good place to start is the company's own website, which will also include its financial reports.
- Websites such as Yahoo! Finance offer excellent comprehensive insights and news, as well as all the metrics listed opposite.
- Most trading platforms also offer individual "company profiles," which are great for research on things such as stock price development and other financials.

 Zoom in

When you start researching, you will see a ton of numbers and it's easy to get overwhelmed. So, focus on the following metrics to become familiar with how you can easily (relatively speaking) analyze and compare companies. Keep in mind,

that companies in different industries typically have fundamental differences, so it can be a little bit like comparing apples to oranges. As mentioned above, all the metrics are widely available on search engines, so you don't need to look far or do any of the math yourself.

In the end you want to answer one question: is the company worth the price that the stock costs, or is the stock price too expensive ("overvalued")? So let's look at a few numbers that can help you:

a) Revenue: This is the amount of money a company has made in a given period. It's the first thing you'll see on the income statement in the annual report, which is why it's often referred to as the "top line." While revenue is a very important figure, high revenue doesn't necessarily mean the company is profitable or attractive to invest in. Imagine you started a company that sold $1 bills for 99 cents. This does not leave much room to pay expenses such as salary, and the company would likely make a loss —even if they sold millions of $1 bills.

b) Earnings and earnings per share (EPS) Earnings are also called profit and can be a positive (the company earned money) or negative (the company lost money) value. Even though it might be obvious that a company that loses money is a bad investment, this doesn't have to be true. For example, startups and smaller companies almost always have big losses in the first years of operation, because they invest in growth or product development. Sometimes, this is seen for big companies, too, and it doesn't necessarily mean the company isn't doing well. Even though positive earnings are preferred, negative earnings doesn't have to mean a business isn't doing well.

Another important financial value for you to know and to evaluate companies is earnings per share. That means you divide earnings by the number of shares available to trade, and you get earnings per share. This number shows a company's profitability on a per-share basis, which can be a useful way to compare one company to another—but more on that in the next step.

c) Price-earnings ratio (P/E): Finally we come to the point that actually helps you answer the question of whether a stock price is too high compared to other similar companies. This is called the P/E ratio and you calculate it by dividing a company's current stock price by its earnings per share. This measure of a stock's value tells you how much investors are willing to

3

Qualitative research

If quantitative stock research reveals the black-and-white financials of a company's story, qualitative stock research provides a more nuanced picture of its operations and prospects.

Warren Buffett famously said: "Buy into a company because you want to own it, not because you want the stock to go up." That's because when you buy stocks, you purchase a personal stake in a business. As a general rule of thumb, the more you know about the industry, the easier it will be to do the research. In our experience, looking into a brand that you already know and love can actually be quite fun.

Here are some questions to help you screen your potential investments. Let's start with how does the company make money? Sometimes this is obvious, such as a clothing retailer whose main business is selling clothes. Sometimes it's not, such as a fast-food company that derives most of its revenue from selling franchises (such as McDonald's or 7-Eleven), or an electronics firm that relies on providing consumer financing for growth. A good rule of thumb that's served Buffett well is: invest in common-sense companies that you truly understand.

Also see if the company has a competitive advantage. Look for something about the business that

pay to receive $1 of the company's current earnings. It's one of the most-used metrics in assessing how attractive a company is, and almost all trading platforms will display the number on the company's "profile page," so you actually don't have to work this out yourself. The key thing to note is that you can only use the number to compare companies in the same industry. For example, comparing Tesla's P/E to the dating app Bumble's P/E won't tell you anything useful, because the two companies have nothing in common, but comparing Tesla's P/E to Ford's P/E will be a good indication of whether Tesla is overvalued. And (very) generally speaking, the higher the P/E ratio, the more likely it is that a company is overvalued.

makes it difficult to copy. This could be its brand—for example, has the company done cool ad campaigns or does it have a great social media presence? It could also be the way it earns money (its business model), its leadership/founder team, its ability to innovate, or patent ownership—to name a few. The harder it is for competitors to copy, the stronger the competitive advantage.

What could go wrong? This is definitely easier said than done, but it's good to think through different scenarios that might affect the company's stock price in the short term. This could be things like a new product launch failing, or a new competitor quickly getting momentum in the industry, or the CEO quitting. Obviously no one can predict the future, but the more we think ahead, the better prepared we are to weather any storms.

Put your stock research into context

As you can see, there are endless metrics and ratios that investors can use to assess a company's general financial health and calculate the intrinsic value of its stock. But looking solely at a company's revenue or income from a single year or the management team's most recent decisions paints an incomplete picture.

Before you buy any stock, you want to build a well-informed narrative about the company and what factors make it worthy of a long-term partnership. And to do that, context is key. For long-term context, look at historical data. The easiest way to do this is by using search engines like Yahoo! Finance, reviewing the company's annual report (it will always list historical numbers for reference) or clicking on the company profile on your trading platform. And, of course, have a look at the stock price development. Is the stock price as high as ever, or maybe it's at an all-time low? This is all information you should take into consideration.

The above four steps are the approach taken by most longer-term investors who are building up their knowledge of the various goings-on. But since we are not only looking at the company's financial performance, but also want to make sure that it complies with our values, we need to do one more bit of due diligence.

Greenwashing and pinkwashing

These are marketing tactics used by companies to present themselves as socially responsible or supportive of certain causes, while in reality their actions may not align with their claims. Let's take a closer look at each:

Greenwashing: This refers to the deceptive practice of companies exaggerating or falsely promoting their environmental efforts to appear more eco-friendly than they actually are. This can mislead consumers into believing the company is genuinely committed to sustainability when, in fact, they might be engaging in environmentally harmful practices.

Example: VW (Volkswagen).
One of the most notorious examples of greenwashing in recent history is Volkswagen's "Dieselgate." Volkswagen marketed its diesel cars as environmentally friendly with "Clean Diesel" technology, claiming lower emissions and eco-friendliness. However, in 2015 the EPA revealed that VW had installed a "defeat device" in their vehicles, cheating emissions tests and emitting harmful pollutants beyond legal limits during normal driving. The scandal resulted in a global outcry, numerous lawsuits, and a $14.7 billion settlement in the US to compensate affected owners and address environmental damages.

Volkswagen faced severe financial losses and reputational damage.

Pinkwashing: This term has multiple meanings, but most commonly refers to a marketing strategy where companies promote support for the LGBTQ+ community while simultaneously failing to uphold meaningful actions that truly benefit the community. This practice can be seen as opportunistic, aiming to improve the company's public image without genuinely advocating for LGBTQ+ rights.

Example: Every June during Pride month, companies around the world change their logo to rainbow colors and make so-called "Pride activation campaigns" showing how supportive and inclusive they are. These campaigns can be highly profitable and are often used widely for marketing purposes. The problem? Many companies fail to support LGBTQ+ rights the remaining 11 months of the year. There are countless examples of this, one being H&M and Levi's, who brought out exclusive, colorful garments as part of their "Pride collections." However, they were criticized for producing the garments in countries where homosexuality was still illegal. Other examples of pinkwashing include companies such as BMW, who've changed their logo to rainbow colors during Pride month. However, this is only in countries that embrace sexual freedom and not less-tolerant nations such as Russia and Saudi Arabia.

ETHICAL INVESTMENT DUE DILIGENCE

Assuming that the basic due diligence came out positive and you're still interested in buying stock, next you need to check if the company fits your ethical standards and values. Similar to the financial due diligence, the process can be broken down into four steps.

 Plan your research

The first step is to revisit your values chart from pages 56-57, so you know what you're looking for. You may also want to reflect on what potential red flags would be. For example, if equal representation is important to you, a company with only white men in top management would probably be a big no-no.

Finding information

Once you know what you're looking for, it's time to find that information. For publicly traded companies, this is generally much easier, but here are some pointers on where to look:

Company website Go to the website and look for their impact/sustainability reports. You can search for relevant key terms, such as "sustainability," "equality," "carbon dioxide," "diversity," etc. If nothing comes up, that's almost never a good sign. Generally speaking, if companies are going out of their way to invest in great ESG practices, they will be shouting from the rooftops about it. Equally, if the latest update of the sustainability report happened five years ago, that may be a sign that the company is not taking this topic too seriously.

Other useful reports that companies often publish—and in some cases are required to publish—include Modern Slavery Reports, Sustainability Reports, ESG Reports, Responsible Business Partner Reports, and more.

Then click through the company's website and read some of the other information they provide. Often you find company presentations, video messages, promotional videos, and all the press statements that the company has done. Of course, you don't have to read all of it, but it can help to give it a scan and see what's available.

Their website can also give you a holistic view about the company. Many large companies act in various sectors; for example, pharma companies produce a wide range of products. Some are very helpful and amazing medicine, but maybe some other products are actually harmful. Look at the company as a whole; don't get blinded by one product or service.

Most companies make shiny promises in beautiful language, but many of them don't take real action. As a rule of thumb, the more concrete and easy to measure a company's promises are, the better. For example, "we want to increase the amount of women in leadership" is a very weak promise, whereas "we want to increase the amount of women in leadership by 20%" is much better because it is easy to measure whether or not the company succeeded and thereby hold them accountable. It is also a great idea to go back in time and check if the company actually lived up to their promises in the past.

News and external articles On search engines, type in "[Company Name] controversies," "[Company Name] criticism," or "[Company Name] penalties." Remember to search the news to get a broad view on what has happened recently. Make sure the source is credible, as it does happen that companies pay organizations to write favorable articles about them—sometimes even hidden as scientific research.[5]

External ratings on sustainability "Sustainalytics," which is Morningstar's ESG investing branch, is one of many tools that evaluate thousands of companies worldwide on various ESG criteria. The assessments are designed to help investors identify companies that are integrating sustainability into their business strategies and operations and they are a great resource to compare different opportunities against each other.

Top tip: For many consumer goods websites like H&M, VW, etc., make sure to go to the website of the group (so the actual company behind the brand), not the website targeted for consumers. For H&M, instead of visiting www.hm.com, go to www.hmgroup.com and VW's company information can be found at www.volkswagen.com. Don't worry, you don't need to know these by heart, as search engines will suggest these immediately once you start looking for investor-related information on that company.

Organizations and policies Try to find organizations that fight for your values and read to see if they have written something about the company you want to invest in. For example, environmental organizations might have extensive opinions about certain companies,

Investing is like voting with your money.

and workers' unions will publish statements on working conditions. Some fast-fashion companies have hit the headlines for their employment of child workers in remote areas of the world on very little pay.[6] This is not in line with the UN's goals and is surely not improving labor standards around the world in a sustainable way.

Other aspects of labor policies that you can look to also include "zero-hour contracts," "health and safety," "remote work," "whistleblowing," "mental health policies," and "pay transparency." While you might not be able to directly compare data, getting a feel for what businesses or funds investing in stocks are up to can help to decipher how sustainably they're behaving.

Management personality check: Yep, that's important. Admittedly not every company has flamboyant or prominent CEOs such as Tesla's Elon Musk or Amazon's Ex-CEO Jeff Bezos, but make sure to look up the CEO and other senior managers of the company you are interested in

and try to spend a few minutes finding out if that person is—at least as far as you can tell—a decent human being, or has made questionable statements, or is tied to an organization you don't approve of.

As is evident, there are numerous factors to take into account, but fundamentally it all comes down to conducting thorough research. The extent of your research is entirely up to you. Continuously investigate until you feel assured that the company aligns with your values and avoids any objectionable behavior. Keep in mind that there could be biases and aspects you might not appreciate. It's unrealistic to expect a company to score a perfect 100 percent and have a spotless track record without any controversies or criticisms. In the following section, we will explore how to assess your findings.

3 Evaluate

Great, you now have a comprehensive understanding of what this company is involved in, and you might have come across some information that doesn't align with your investment preferences. Simultaneously, you might have discovered commendable initiatives undertaken by the company. For instance, it could be lacking in sustainability efforts, but excels in female leadership and worker rights.

It's time to evaluate and rank how well the company aligns with your investment preferences. A straightforward approach is to assign a score to each value that holds significance for you. You could rate the company on a scale of 1 to 10, with 1 representing poor performance and 10 indicating excellence. Realistically, most scores will fall in between extreme values.

Pay close attention to any red flags you encounter—these should be immediate deal-breakers. For instance, if labor rights are of utmost importance to you and you find that the company plans to cut salaries and move operations to areas known for exploiting cheap labor, this is an absolute no-go. Similarly, if the company profits significantly by selling to dictatorships, it could be a critical factor to reconsider investing.

Once you have assessed and scored the company, you can tally the points. This evaluation serves as a guideline to compare different options. Depending on your priorities, you may weigh certain scores more heavily in your overall assessment. However, as a general rule, we recommend that your chosen company should score at least 60 percent of all possible points you have assigned to ensure it meets your investment criteria.

Comparing apples to oranges

When analyzing various investment prospects, it's crucial to avoid comparing apples to oranges. Hence, it's vital to identify companies that are comparable in the aspect you are assessing. For instance, if you are evaluating two companies based on their carbon emissions, make sure that they operate within the same industry and are approximately similar in terms of revenue scale. For instance, a shipping company will naturally exhibit a considerably larger carbon footprint than a software company. Similarly, a local online bookstore will inherently possess a far smaller carbon footprint than Amazon.

Don't make rushed decisions, and if you feel you need to do more research, do so. In the end it is all about what makes you feel comfortable.

Make a verdict

Now that you have your scores, it's time for your final judgement. As the sole decision maker, examine the individual scores of the values, then consider the overall total. Additionally, take into account your existing investments and how this new company fits within your broader portfolio. For instance, if your current portfolio comprises several companies focused on carbon neutrality while the one you are assessing excels in gender equality but lags in carbon neutrality, it could be a good way to diversify. Ultimately, this decision boils down to your personal preferences and strategy.

If you're not completely satisfied with either the financial or ethical due diligence, consider changing your usual investment amount. For example, instead of investing $1,000, you might choose to invest only $500. Trust your judgement, but keep in mind, that despite doing extensive research, it is impossible to know every minute detail about a company.

Impressive! That was indeed a lot to consider, but don't be daunted by the due diligence process. It may seem like a substantial task, but conducting desktop research won't take much time. However, avoid making rushed decisions; if you feel the need for more research, go ahead and explore further. In the end, it's all about finding your comfort level. Spend some time investigating, and if after an hour you can't find any negative articles about, let's say, pollution, perhaps the company is doing well in that aspect. Conversely, if you uncover multiple court cases involving worker exploitation within the first five minutes of googling, it's probably best to consider it a pass.

Remember, conducting due diligence is not a one-time event. Regularly reassess your investments, both financially and ethically. Companies can change, for better or worse. Spend a few minutes every now and then checking for any negative news, new product developments, competition, and recent financials. If you're content with what you find, that's fantastic. However, if you discover something unsettling, you may want to reconsider your investment in the company. Stay informed and stay vigilant to ensure your investments align with your values.

Key takeaways

Having a strategy—and sticking to it—is key to becoming a successful long-term investor. When it comes to impact investing, having a strategy helps you make informed, conscious decisions. This chapter has covered three strategies:

- **Do no harm:** Removing all investments that can objectively be classified as "harmful."
- **Impact only:** Only investing in companies that live up to your basic impact standards.
- **Maximum impact:** Only investing in companies that actively work to make the world a better place.

What else can you do to change the world?

Starting something *yourself*

You've now learned how to make money by investing in companies or projects that solve a problem you care about. But what should you do if you can't find a company or organization that's tackling the problem that matters so much to you? And what if they aren't doing it right?

One option that many people overlook is the opportunity to start something yourself. This could be a company, organization, movement, NGO, or something completely different. Regardless of what you start, it will require effort, time, and sacrifice beyond anything else in this book. But the potential to truly change the world is also that much bigger. Trust us, we've been there while building Female Invest.

In this chapter, we'll share our best advice for making an impact in alternative ways. Whether by starting your own organization, getting politically involved, or mentoring someone in your community.

BE THE CHANGE YOU WANT TO SEE

By starting a company or project yourself, you can be the change you want to see in the world. You have the power to shape your vision into a tangible reality, while at the same time driving positive transformation in your chosen field.

Here's why:

Freedom to pursue your passion: Launching your own venture allows you to tackle issues that truly matter to you. You have the freedom to focus on a cause or a problem you're deeply passionate about, enabling you to pour your energy and creativity into finding innovative solutions. This personal connection and dedication can drive you to make a lasting impact.

Flexibility to shape your values: When you start something yourself, you have the opportunity to build a business or project that reflects your values. From the company culture to the products or services you offer, you can embed sustainability, social responsibility, or any other principles you hold dear. By aligning your vision with your values, you can create a positive impact that extends beyond financial gains.

Ability to inspire and empower others: Your initiative can serve as a catalyst for change, inspiring others to follow their own passions and make a difference themselves. By demonstrating the possibilities and sharing your own journey, you can empower individuals, communities, and even industries to embrace positive transformation.

WHAT TO CONSIDER WHEN GOING SOLO

When starting something yourself, here are three essential considerations:

Clear purpose and mission: Define the purpose and mission of your venture, ensuring that it aligns with the positive change you seek. A well-defined purpose will guide your decision-making and inspire others to join your cause.

Strategic planning and execution: Develop a comprehensive plan that outlines your goals, your target audience, resources, and growth strategy. Prioritize action steps and be adaptable to navigate any challenges that you might encounter along the way.

Collaborate and network: Forge partnerships with like-minded individuals, organizations, and stakeholders. Collaboration amplifies your impact, allows for knowledge sharing, and fosters a supportive community of change-makers.

Remember, starting something yourself requires perseverance, adaptability, and a willingness to learn from setbacks. But with passion, dedication, and a down-to-earth approach, you can create a venture that contributes positively to the world.

GETTING STARTED

There are many opinions about how best to start something yourself. Some people believe you need unique knowledge and experience, while others believe you just need a great idea. While there are many ways to Rome, we believe you need two things: passion and grit. That's because, in the end, a good idea is not enough. If you want to change the world with your company, organization, or movement you'll need a burning passion and a will to give up time and comfort. While people with access to network and capital, or people, might have an easier time getting their idea off the ground, we believe anyone can start something themselves.

Before launching into your project, here are a few considerations:

You don't need to go full-time right away
Despite what stereotypes might suggest, you don't need to go full-time on your idea from the off. Even though working more hours would be ideal, the reality is that most founders stay in their day job so that they can pay the bills until their company starts taking off.

Surround yourself with people who support you
While listening to feedback is good, surrounding yourself with people who support you is key. Starting something yourself isn't easy, and you'll need emotional support along the way.

Think big, but take small steps
Rome wasn't built in a day and neither is a world-changing organization/company/movement. Even though it's important to be ambitious and think big, you also need to remember to be careful and to take one step at a time to make sure you build a solid foundation.

Find a way to make money
This might be controversial, but we truly believe that the more money you make, the bigger an impact you can have. While women are severely under-represented in the founding of for-profit companies, they are over-represented in the nonprofit sector.[1] It's time for women to step into the for-profit world and accept the notion that you can make money while making a difference (and for the world to accept and support women making money).

Other options

This book is about making the world a better place, and while it focuses on investing, there are other ways of doing this. We've gathered a few here for inspiration.

- **Mentor someone in your space**—The guidance of someone who is higher up in a profession, who has obtained a certain qualification, or who has strong expertise in a particular area, can make a huge difference to the next generation of workers.
- **Work for a company with a strong social cause**—You've got approximately 80,000 hours to make a difference in your career (based on 40 hours per week, 50 weeks per year, for 40 years). That's a lot of time you could use to further the efforts of a company that's trying to make the world a better place.[2]
- **Petitions**—This is a quick win. Take a few moments of your time to sign petitions for causes that you believe in and that might drive those in positions of power to make

changes to the world that are much needed.

- **Stewardship**—Use your voice to encourage and lobby for ethical decision-making and investing among companies. Look into what their ESG policies are and if you don't like what you see, write to them. Speaking up is powerful.
- **Political donations**—Over half of the countries in the world allow unlimited donations to political campaigns.[3] While this in itself has lots of potentially negative implications, try to counter it with the positive influences. By donating time or money to candidates or certain political parties that are championing doing good in the world, you can help them to get their voices heard.[4]
- **Protesting**—If you live in a country where protests are permitted, you might feel comfortable to go out there and campaign for the causes that you believe in to influence bigger powers. This costs nothing and may well influence decisions.

Did you know?

Often people think of lobbying and protesting as "a hobby for hippies," which might put off some. Terms like "tree hugging" get bandied around in an attempt to diminish the work of protesters. But if we look back to the origins of this term, it was actually Indian women who we have to thank for it; the Chipko movement in the early 1970s saw local women in the Indian Himalayas stand by fourteen ash trees to stop the sports company Symonds from cutting them down. They stood holding, or rather hugging, the trees so that the large machinery could not cut down the trees as planned. A ban on felling the trees was eventually upheld for decades following the actions of these brave women. A simple hug can be very effective. Female power in action![5]

Look at your life and consider where you can make a positive contribution to the world.

Time is money; *are you spending yours in the best way?*

Economists have developed a theory on how much of our time we're willing to exchange for money. The general conclusion is that there is an optimum balance of time and pay. Following this idea, people are willing to exchange more of their time for being paid more, but this has a limit—we all need sleep and at some point we probably want to spend some of the money that is being earned from the many hours of working, outside of work. After this optimum point, more money doesn't mean more hours are worked, because the currency of time outweighs the benefits of receiving more money. Check out the chart for the visuals.[6]

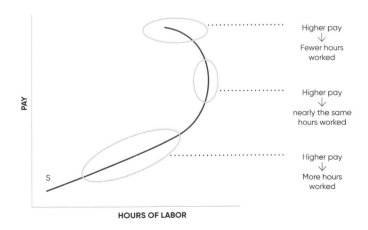

PAY

Higher pay
↓
Fewer hours
worked

Higher pay
↓
nearly the same
hours worked

Higher pay
↓
More hours
worked

S

HOURS OF LABOR

Have you heard of the $75k hypothesis?

There's tons of research that suggests that having more money doesn't actually make you happier. The $75k hypothesis is a theory based around the idea that once you earn more than $75k, your happiness doesn't increase all that much[7]—you're already relatively comfortable, and you can afford to buy the things that you need and want.

Interestingly, happiness with money is not just about the amount you have, but also how you got it. Research shows that millionaires who made the money themselves are happier than those who inherited it or married into it. Crucially, the happiest millionaires are the ones who are self-made and who give the majority of their fortune away. Through donating, investing, and philanthropy, the generous millionaires reach the highest levels of satisfaction.[8]

Key takeaways

Changing the world is no small task, and there are many ways to have a positive impact. This book has focused on investing, but if you don't have the money, there are other actions to consider.

- **Starting something yourself:** If you can't find a company that solves the problem you care about, starting a company/organization/movement yourself is an option. It's a huge, life-changing task, but it holds potential for limitless impact.
- **Other options:** Work for a company with a strong social cause, mentor someone in your space, sign petitions, and get politically involved.
- **Take responsibility:** We all have a role to play and a chance to make a difference, whether this is through investments, conscious shopping, mentorship, political involvement, or emotional support toward those fighting our battles. Look at your life, and consider where you can make a positive contribution to the world—no matter how small it is.

You've finished the book— *now what?*

Well done!

You've just finished reading a book on a topic that's notorious for being dry and complicated. From understanding the complexity of impact investments and their potential, to learning tangible methods for implementing your knowledge in the real world, we hope that this book has shown you that impact investing is possible—and that you don't have to be rich to make an impact with your money.

We also hope that this book has shown you that:

- Impact investing has the potential to change the world.
- You can get started even with small amounts.
- Anyone can make a difference with their money.

We need to redefine what making a difference with money looks like by moving away from the traditional notion of "just" donating money and time. Because even though this is great, you can only spend your time and money once, which limits your impact. There are no quick solutions to solving pressing social and environmental issues, and impact investing is not a perfect fix. But it's a whole lot better than sitting on the sidelines, watching the world burn.

Impact investing is not a perfect fix. But it's a whole lot better than sitting on the sidelines, watching the world burn.

MAKING MONEY WHILE MAKING A DIFFERENCE

Money is power, and we need to start acting like it. For far too long, women have been under-represented in high-powered networks, while at the same time being over-represented in nonprofit organizations, volunteering work, and unpaid care work. Those things are important, but the burden shouldn't fall disproportionately on women, ultimately keeping them from making money and influencing large-scale decisions within climate, social justice, and the future of the planet.

It's time to normalize women making money while making a difference. It's time for women to own their financial power, and it's time for society to encourage and support them. Because if women start to use their financial power, it can unleash change like we've never seen before. We can't leave the full responsibility for change with the leaders of our world. Instead, we all need to show leadership in our own world and local communities. We have the money. We have the knowledge. We have the opportunity. Let's use it.

The best time to start?
Yesterday.

The second-best time to start?
Today.

LET'S CHANGE THE FUTURE

Women have historically been excluded from positions of power. To this day, they remain severely under-represented at the top of governments and companies where decisions about the future of humanity are being made. Ironically, women are more efficient in acting on climate change and social injustice, and countries and companies with more women at the top generally have more ambitious climate and social policies.[1,2] At the same time, women are hit harder by the consequences of climate change and financial volatility.

Irreversible damage will be done to our planet long before women achieve equal representation. The UN estimates it will take 140 years to achieve equal representation.[3] Scientists warn we have 8 years to avoid climate catastrophe.[4] We simply can't afford to wait. It's time to step into our financial power and use money to change the world.

Money is power.

Are you ready to use yours?

Glossary

ALTERNATIVE INVESTMENTS: Alternative investments refer to investment options that fall outside of traditional asset classes like stocks, bonds, and cash. These investments are considered non-traditional and often have unique characteristics, risk-return profiles, and investment strategies. Examples of alternative investments include private equity, venture capital, hedge funds, real estate, commodities, infrastructure projects, collectables (such as art or wine), and cryptocurrencies. These assets offer diversification and potential for higher returns, but often come with higher risks and less liquidity compared to traditional investments.

ANGEL INVESTOR: An angel investor, also known as a private investor or seed investor, is an individual who provides capital and support to early-stage startups or entrepreneurs in exchange for equity ownership or a stake in the company.

BLOCKCHAIN: A decentralized technology that powers most cryptocurrencies. Blockchain facilitates exchanges of information between people, such as payments, but without using any middleman, like a bank. Blockchain technology uses cryptography—very complex mathematical code—to secure the system.

BONDS: Represent a loan made by an investor to a borrower—typically a company or government. The borrower pays investors a fixed return rate for a fixed period of time. Unlike stocks, bonds don't give any ownership rights.

COMMODITIES: Commodities are basic goods that can be transformed into other goods and services.

COMPOUND INTEREST: Much like a snowball effect, this is interest earned on money that was previously earned as interest. Also known as exponential growth.

CROWDFUNDING: When people—"the crowd"—are given the opportunity to invest in an unlisted company (not listed on a stock market), such as a startup. It allows businesses to turn community members into shareholders, who stand to profit should the business do well.

CRYPTOCURRENCY: Cryptocurrencies—or crypto—are digital or virtual currencies that don't exist in any physical form, but live only on a computer network. The most well-known cryptocurrency is Bitcoin.

CURRENCY: A generally accepted form of payment, typically issued by a government. Most countries have their own currency—such as the US dollar or the Japanese yen. In general, currency is crucial for facilitating trades across countries and works because every nation agrees that paper notes and coins have an inherent value, meaning we can use them to purchase goods.

CYCLICAL/NON-CYCLICAL: Cyclicality is a term used to describe how a company (and hence a stock) is affected by development in the global economy. A cyclical stock will be more affected by the state of the economy, while non-cyclical stocks are less affected.

DIVERSIFICATION: The process of spreading out your risk in an attempt to combat market volatility by investing in a range of different companies, across different regions, sectors, and countries.

DIVIDEND: A way of earning money through investing, where regular payments are made to shareholders out of the company's revenue, typically quarterly or annually.

DUE DILIGENCE: Due diligence refers to the comprehensive investigation and analysis conducted by an individual or organization before entering into a business transaction or making an investment. It is a crucial process that aims to gather relevant information and assess the potential risks and benefits associated with the transaction or investment.

ETF: Exchange-Traded Fund—a fund traded directly on the exchange. ETFs are different than other funds, as they are traded throughout the day. They are made up of a variety of investments, including commodities, stocks, bonds, or a mixture of investment types.

EPS: EPS stands for Earnings Per Share. It is a financial metric that measures the profitability of a company by dividing its net earnings (profits) by the total number of outstanding shares of its common stock. EPS is a key indicator used by investors, analysts, and shareholders to assess a company's profitability on a per-share basis.

ESG FUNDS: ESG stands for Environmental, Social, and Governance. An ESG fund is a type of investment fund that integrates these three factors into its investment strategy. The fund's goal is to not only generate financial returns for investors, but also consider the environmental impact, social responsibility, and corporate governance practices of the companies it invests in.

EXCHANGE: Stocks are traded on an online stock exchange where companies and investors issue stocks to trade. Stocks are priced according to supply and demand. To trade stocks through the stock exchange, you need to access them through a trading app.

FUNDS: In the context of investments, the term "funds" refers to investment vehicles or financial products that pool together capital from multiple investors to invest in various assets. Funds can take different forms, such as mutual funds, exchange-traded funds (ETFs), hedge funds, or private equity funds.

FUND MANAGER: Responsible for a fund's investment strategy and for managing its portfolio. A fund can be managed by one or two people, or by a team of many managers, depending on the size of the fund, and incurs a fee to do so.

INDEX: Used to track the performance of a certain type of stock, a specific sector, or a country's stock market. An example is the S&P 500 Index, which tracks the performance of the 500 largest companies listed on the US stock exchange.

INFLATION: This is the rate by which overall prices within an economy increase. Due to inflation, our money slowly loses value, which means you're losing purchasing power.

INTEREST RATE: When taking out a loan, the interest rate is the amount of money a lender receives for lending out money to you. This is typically expressed as an annual percentage rate (APR). When saving money, the interest rate applies to the amount earned at a bank from a savings account.

IMPACT INVESTING: Impact investing refers to an investment approach that seeks to generate both financial returns and positive social or environmental impact. It goes beyond traditional financial metrics and aims to address specific social or environmental challenges through investment activities.

IPO: Initial Public Offering—when a company initially makes stocks available to individual investors, who can proceed to buy stocks in the company.

P/E RATIO: Price-to-Earnings value—investors use this metric to decide if a stock is under- or overvalued and to evaluate the price of the stock compared to other companies in its industry. The P/E ratio is calculated by dividing the price per share by the company's earnings per share. For example, if a company's P/E ratio is 25, it means that its stocks are traded at 25 times its earnings. A high P/E does not always mean that a company is overvalued, and a low P/E does not always mean that a company is undervalued. The P/E should therefore not be the only thing you consider, but it can be a good indication of how attractive the stock is.

PORTFOLIO: Simply put, your portfolio refers to the basket of investments you own, across stocks, bonds, and investment funds. So if you own three stocks, your portfolio consists of three stocks.

REIT: Stands for "Real Estate Investment Trust." If you want to invest in property, but are not in a position to buy a full property yourself, then you can buy shares in REITs. These are companies that own and often operate a collection of properties—and any profits from rent, or increases in value, are shared among the shareholders.

RETURN: The money you accrue through investing. You can get returns in two ways: 1) When you sell a stock at a higher price than you bought it for, and 2) When you receive stock dividends, which is when a company decides to share benefits of its progress.

SCOPES 1, 2, AND 3: Scope 1, Scope 2, and Scope 3 are terms commonly used in the context of greenhouse gas (GHG) emissions accounting and management. They represent different categories of emissions sources for an organization or entity.

SDGs: SDGs, or Sustainable Development Goals, are a set of 17 global goals established by the United Nations in 2015. These goals provide a blueprint for addressing pressing social, economic, and environmental challenges and achieving sustainable development worldwide by the year 2030.

SFDR: SFDR, or the Sustainable Finance Disclosure Regulation, is a regulatory framework implemented in the European Union (EU) aimed at enhancing transparency and promoting sustainability in the financial sector.

SECURITIES: Different types of financial assets that hold some kind of monetary value and can be traded. A stock is an example of a security.

STOCKS/SHARES: Stocks represent ownership of a company. When you buy a stock, you own a share in the company. Companies issue stocks to investors as a way to raise money to fund growth, products, and other initiatives.

STOP-LOSS/TRAILING STOP-LOSS: A tool provided by most trading platforms to ensure that your investment is automatically sold. Stop-loss comes in two different variations: stop-loss and trailing stop-loss. **Stop-loss:** your investment is automatically sold once it hits a certain price decided by you. **Trailing stop-loss:** you decide a percentage decrease that will trigger the stop-loss to sell.

SUSTAINABLE INVESTING: Sustainable investing, also known as socially responsible investing (SRI) or sustainable finance, refers to an investment approach that takes into account environmental, social, and governance (ESG) factors when making investment decisions. The goal of sustainable investing is to generate long-term financial returns while also promoting sustainable and responsible practices.

THE FIVE Ps: The "Five Ps" refers to a framework commonly used in sustainable and impact investing to evaluate investments based on five key dimensions: People, Planet, Prosperity, Peace, and Partnerships. This framework recognizes the interconnectedness of social, environmental, and economic factors in achieving sustainable development.

TIME HORIZON: Time is a crucial factor to consider when investing. Your time horizon is essentially the time you want to keep your investments. As a rule of thumb, you're a long-term investor if your time horizon is more than five years (or 10 or 30). A short time horizon is less than five years.

TRADING ACCOUNT: The main tool used by investors to invest. It offers access to stocks on the open exchange which you can buy and sell accordingly.

VOLATILITY: How stable a security or market is. When the price is relatively stable, the security has low volatility. If the security has dramatic increases and unexpected falls, the security has high volatility.

References

Intro

1   Data from: "Percentage of the population in England who gave to charity from 2013/14 to 2021/22, by gender" - https://www.statista.com/statistics/292929/giving-to-charity-in-england-by-gender/

2   https://www.civilsociety.co.uk/voices/daniel-fluskey-women-give-more-than-men-to-charity-but-why.html

3   https://teamkinetic.co.uk/blog/2019/07/10/women-volunteer-more-than-men/

4   Managing the Next Decade of Women's Wealth, April 9th 2020, Boston Consulting Group (BCG); https://www.bcg.com/publications/2020/managing-next-decade-women-wealth

5   Astghik Mavisakalyan, Yashar Tarverdi, Gender and climate change: Do female parliamentarians make difference? European Journal of Political Economy, Volume 56, 2019, Pages 151-164, ISSN 0176-2680, https://doi.org/10.1016/j.ejpoleco.2018.08.001(https://www.sciencedirect.com/science/article/pii/S0176268017304500)

6   https://www.kcl.ac.uk/news/women-political-leaders-key-to-more-equal-and-caring-societies

7   https://www.fool.com/research/women-in-investing-research/

8   https://www.unep.org/climate-emergency

9   William J Ripple and others, World Scientists' Warning of a Climate Emergency, BioScience, Volume 70, Issue 1, January 2020, Pages 8–12, https://doi.org/10.1093/biosci/biz088

10 Women's Forum 2021 G20 Barometer on gender equity: https://events.womens-forum.com/womens-forum/documents/b6394609-6e07-ed11-b47a-281878664f63/2021-g20-barometer-on-gender-equity

11 https://climatechampions.unfccc.int/the-climate-crisis-cannot-wait-for-men-to-act-we-need-women-at-the-top-table-now/

12 https://climatechampions.unfccc.int/the-climate-crisis-cannot-wait-for-men-to-act-we-need-women-at-the-top-table-now/

13. Data from: "Number of countries where the de facto highest position of executive power was held by a woman from 1960 to 2023" - https://www.statista.com/statistics/1058345/countries-withwomen-highest-position-executivepower-since-1960/
14. https://www.catalyst.org/research/women-ceos-of-the-sp-500/
15. https://www.unwomen.org/en/news-stories/explainer/2022/02/explainer-how-gender-inequality-and-climate-change-are-interconnected
16. https://www.ohchr.org/en/stories/2022/07/climate-change-exacerbates-violence-against-women-and-girls
17. https://news.un.org/en/story/2021/11/1105322
18. https://devinit.org/resources/inequality-global-trends/
19. Chancel, L., Piketty, T., Saez, E., Zucman, G. et al. World Inequality Report 2022, World Inequality Lab. https://wid.world/document/world-inequality-report-2022/
20. Chancel, L., Piketty, T., Saez, E., Zucman, G. et al. World Inequality Report 2022, World Inequality Lab. https://wid.world/document/world-inequality-report-2022/
21. Sustainable Funds U.S. Landscape Report, Feb. 2020. https://www.morningstar.com/sustainable-investing/broken-record-flows-us-sustainable-funds-again-reach-new-heights
22. Keynes, J.M. (1930). A Treatise on Money. Volume I
23. https://www.history.co.uk/shows/mankind-the-story-of-all-of-us/articles/the-history-of-money
24. https://www.nationalgeographic.com/history/article/worlds-oldest-coin-factory-discovered-in-china
25. https://www.eurochange.co.uk/travel/tips/world-currency-abbreviations-symbols-and-codes-travel-money
26. https://www.fraserinstitute.org/sites/default/files/is-climate-catastrophe-really-10-years-away.pdf

Chapter 1

1. Global Impact Investing Network, https://thegiin.org/impact-investing/need-to-know/#what-is-impact-investing
2. BlackRock, https://www.blackrock.com/uk/solutions/sustainable-investing
3. Sustainable Finance and Impact Investing – Any Difference? https://www.linkedin.com/pulse/sustainable-finance-impact-investing-any-difference-dr-hakan-lucius/
4. Data from: dbSustainability - Are we at an inflection point for a major advance in ESG fund launches? September 2021. Fig. 9 (source: Morningstar Direct, Deutsche Bank).
5. RBC Wealth Management, https://www.rbcwealthmanagement.com/en-us/newsroom/2021-04-06/women-are-leading-the-charge-for-environmental-social-and-governance-esg-investing-in-the-us-amid-growing-demand-for-responsible-investing-solutions
6. https://www.fool.com/investing/stock-market/types-of-stocks/esg-investing/
7. https://sdgs.un.org/goals
8. https://education.nationalgeographic.org/resource/sustainable-development-goals
9. https://www.iberdrola.com/sustainability/committed-sustainable-development-goals/what-is-agenda-2030
10. https://www.eurosif.org/policies/sfdr/
11. European Union, https://eur-lex.europa.eu/legal-content/EN/TXT/?uri=CELEX:32019R2088
12. https://www.ft.com/content/4800d071-0464-4d15-ba32-a47d9f35b77b
13. https://finance.ec.europa.eu/system/files/2021-04/sustainable-finance-taxonomy-faq_en.pdf
14. EU Taxonomy User Guide – a simple guide on the Taxonomy for non-experts, https://ec.europa.eu/sustainable-finance-taxonomy

Chapter 2

1. *Explanation: The 500 largest publicly listed companies in the US
2. https://www.ga-institute.com/nc/storage/press-releases/article/92-of-sp-500r-companies-and-70-of-russell-1000r-companies-published-sustainability-reports-in-202.html
3. https://www.corporateknights.com/rankings/global-100-rankings/2023-global-100-rankings/2023-global-100-most-sustainable-companies/
4. https://www.vox.com/future-perfect/2019/7/16/20694781/volkswagen-emissions-cheating-pollution-child-health

5   https://www.forbes.com/sites/
    georgkell/2022/12/05/from-emissions-
    cheater-to-climate-leader-vws-journey-
    from-dieselgate-to-embracing-e-
    mobility/?sh=70e3a1db68a5
6   https://www.theguardian.com.
    business/2015/sep/22/vw-scandal-
    caused-nearly-1m-tonnes-of-extra-
    pollution-analysis-shows
7   https://www.volkswagenag.com/en/
    news/2019/03/VW_Group_JPK_19.html
8   https://www.greenpeace.org/usa/
    wp-content/uploads/legacy/Global/usa/
    planet3/publications/gwe/2010/BP%20
    bad%20behavior.pdf
9   https://changingmarkets.org/wp-content/
    uploads/2022/06/Greenwash.
    com-packaging-press-release.pdf
10 https://www.breakfreefromplastic.
    org/2022/11/15/the-coca-cola-company-
    named-worst-plastic-polluter-for-five-
    years-in-a-row-brand-audit-2022-report
11 https://www.greenpeace.org/aotearoa/
    press-release/coca-colas-latest-
    greenwashing-an-attempt-at-disguising-
    its-biggest-polluter-status/
12 https://www.oecd.org/environment/plastic-
    pollution-is-growing-relentlessly-as-waste-
    management-and-recycling-fall-short.htm
13 https://www.oecd.org/environment/plastic-
    pollution-is-growing-relentlessly-as-waste-
    management-and-recycling-fall-short.htm
14 https://www.theguardian.com/
    environment/2022/oct/04/cop27-
    climate-summit-sponsorship-polluter-
    coca-cola-condemned-as-greenwash
15 https://www.theguardian.com/environment/
    2020/nov/15/australian-farm-to-hold-
    50000-crocodiles-for-luxury-hermes-goods-
    questioned-by-animal-welfare-groups
16 https://www.worldanimalprotection.org/
    news/australian-crocodiles-be-cruelly-
    slaughtered-new-hermes-farm-0
17 https://www.businessinsider.com/
    fast-fashion-environmental-impact-
    pollution-emissions-waste-water-2019-
    10?r=US&IR=T
18 https://www.business-humanrights.org/en/
    latest-news/usa-hm-faces-greenwashing-
    class-action-lawsuit-over-alleged-
    misleading-false-marketing-of-
    sustainable-clothing-line/

19 https://fashionunited.uk/news/fashion/h-m-
    accused-of-burning-12-tonnes-of-new-
    unsold-clothing-per-
    year/2017101726341
20 https://www.pmi.com/who-we-are/
    who-we-are-overview
21 https://www.cdc.gov/tobacco/data_
    statistics/fact_sheets/health_effects/
    tobacco_related_mortality/index.html

Chapter 3

1   The Values Compass, Dr. Mandeep Rai
2   The Values Compass, Dr. Mandeep Rai
3   https://www.antislavery.org/slavery-today/
    modern-slavery/#:~:text=According%20
    to%20the%20latest%20Global,of%20
    modern%20slavery%20are%20children
4   Global Estimates of Modern Slavery:
    Forced Labour and Forced Marriage,
    International Labour Organization (ILO),
    Walk Free, and International Organization
    for Migration (IOM), Geneva, 2022;
    https://cdn.walkfree.org/content/
    uploads/2022/09/12142341/
    GEMS-2022_Report_EN_V8.pdf
5   https://www.kff.org/global-health-policy/
    fact-sheet/the-global-hivaids-
    epidemic/#:~:text=Approximately%20
    84%20million%20people%20
    have,the%20start%20of%20the%20
    epidemic.&text=Today%2C%20there%20
    are%20approximately%2038,the%20
    beginning%20of%20the%20epidemic.
6   Global estimates of modern slavery: Forced
    labour and forced marriage, International
    Labour Office (ILO), Geneva, 2017;https://
    www.ilo.org/wcmsp5/groups/public/@
    dgreports/@dcomm/documents/
    publication/wcms_575479.pdf
7   https://www.cbsnews.com/news/
    la-garment-factories-investigation/
8   https://www.qardus.com/news/
    halal-investment-a-beginners-guide

Chapter 4

1   Women & Financial Wellness: Beyond the
    Bottom Line, A Merrill Lynch Study,
    Conducted In Partnership With Age
    Wave; https://financialallianceforwomen.
    org/download/women-financial-wellness-
    beyond-bottom-line/)

Chapter 5

1   https://www.oecd.org/financial/education/launchoftheoecdinfeglo balfinancialliteracy surveyreport.htm

2   https://www.oecd.org/financial/education/launchoftheoecdinfeglobalfinancial literacy surveyreport.htm

3   https://tulipshare.com/how-it-works

4   https://twitter.com/KylieJenner/status/966429897118728192?ref_ src=twsrc%5Etfw%7Ctwcamp%5 Etweete mbed%7Ctwterm% 5E966429 8971187281 92%7Ctwgr%5E5985223ae 67916e8c4299 d7d875c37d7737604fd% 7Ctwcon%5Es1_ &ref_url=https%3A%2F %2Fwww.vogue.com%2Farticle%2Fkylie-jenner-tweet-snapchat-stock-fall

5   https://seekingalpha.com/article/4502739-average-stock-market-return

6   https://seekingalpha.com/article/4502739-average-stock-market-return

7   https://eu.patagonia.com/gb/en/activism/

8   https://www.burberryplc.com/en/responsibility/communities/ongoing-initiatives-and-policies.html

9   https://www.forbes.com/advisor/investing/what-is-a-bond/

10 https://www.forbes.com/advisor/investing/what-is-a-bond/

11 US Securities and Exchange Commission, Bonds, https://www.investor.gov/introduction-investing/investing-basics/investment-products/bonds-or-fixed-income-products/bonds

12 US Securities and Exchange Commission, Stocks, https://www.investor.gov/introduction-investing/investing-basics/investment-products/stocks

13 The World Bank Impact Report 2020 https://issuu.com/jlim5/docs/world-bank-ibrd-impact-report-2020?mode=window

14 Nasdaq Green Bond Criteria, https://www.nasdaq.com/docs/Nasdaq-Green-Bond-Criteria_v2.pdf

15 https://www.santander.com/en/stories/what-are-green-bonds

16 https://www.ishares.com/us/products/305296/ishares-usd-green-bond-etf

17 https://iixglobal.com/the-orange-bond-principles-a-new-model-for-investing-in-women-dfc-gov/

Chapter 6

1   https://www.investopedia.com/terms/c/crowdfunding.asp

2   https://www.beauhurst.com/blog/uk-equity-crowdfunding/

3   https://hbr.org/2023/02/for-female-founders-only-fundraising-from-female-vcs-comes-at-a-cost

4   https://www.beauhurst.com/blog/uk-equity-crowdfunding/

5   https://www.ft.com/content/a4336c48-0976-42a3-9a75-58ab334c41f3

6   https://techcrunch.com/2022/10/21/black-startup-founders-raised-just-187-million-in-the-third-quarter/

7   Agrawal, Ajay, et al. "Some Simple Economics of Crowdfunding." Innovation Policy and the Economy, vol. 14, no. 1, 2014, pp. 63–97. JSTOR, https://doi.org/10.1086/ 674021. Accessed 10 Oct. 2022.

8   https://www.beauhurst.com/blog/uk-equity-crowdfunding/

9   https://www.crowdcube.com/explore/investing/tax-relief

10 https://femalefounderspace.com/5-crowdfunding-campaigns-of-female-founders-and-their-key-to-success/

11 https://ncnean.com/pages/why-do-we-exist

12 https://www.embroker.com/blog/startup-statistics/

13 https://www.asa.org.uk/news/asa-enforcement-notice-continues-clampdown-on-misleading-and-irresponsible-crypto-ads.html

14 https://www.wired.co.uk/article/ethereum-merge-big-deal-crypto-environment

15 https://hbr.org/2021/05/how-much-energy-does-bitcoin-actually-consume

16 https://www.nytimes.com/2022/11/22/nyregion/crypto-mining-ban-hochul.html#:~:text=New %20York%20became%20the%20first,over% 20the%20energy%2Dintensive%20activity.

17 https://content.ftserussell.com/sites/default/files/education_proof_of_stake_paper_v6_0.pdf

18 https://www.businessinsider.com/afghanistan-women-turn-to-cryptocurrency-to-feed-their-families-2022-1?r=US&IR=T

19   Europol (2021), Cryptocurrencies - Tracing the evolution of criminal finances, Europol Spotlight Report series, Publications Office of the European Union, Luxembourg; https://www.europol.europa.eu/cms/sites/default/files/documents/Europol%20Spotlight%20-%20Cryptocurrencies%20-%20Tracing%20the%20evolution%20of%20criminal%20finances.pdf

20   https://www.nytimes.com/2022/12/13/technology/john-j-ray-iii-ftx-chief-executive.html

21   https://www.coindesk.com/business/2022/11/02/divisions-in-sam-bankman-frieds-crypto-empire-blur-on-his-trading-titan-alamedas-balance-sheet/

22   https://time.com/6243086/ftx-where-did-money-go/

23   https://www.nytimes.com/2022/12/13/technology/john-j-ray-iii-ftx-chief-executive.html

24   https://www.british-business-bank.co.uk/finance-hub/angel-investment/

25   https://corporatefinanceinstitute.com/resources/knowledge/finance/what-is-angel-investor/

26   https://www.forbes.com/sites/geristengel/2022/10/12/share-of-angel-funding-for-female-startup-ceos-drops-despite-surge-in-dollars/?sh=4813a8815805

27   https://www.forbes.com/sites/geristengel/2022/08/03/women-angel-investors-a-movement-that-has-taken-off/?sh=f13bafa2a18f

28   https://scholars.unh.edu/cgi/viewcontent.cgi?article=1535&context=honors

29   Henry, Annie V., "Exploring the Gender-Based Funding Gap in the Global Angel Investing Market" (2020). Honors Theses and Capstones. 519. https://scholars.unh.edu/honors/519

30   https://corporatefinanceinstitute.com/resources/knowledge/finance/what-is-angel-investor/

31   https://www.upcounsel.com/how-much-do-angel-investors-usually-invest#:~:text=From%20Angel%20Investors-,How%20much%20do%20angel%20investors%20usually%20invest%3F,often%20friends%20or%20family%20members.

32   https://www.british-business-bank.co.uk/wp-content/uploads/2018/06/Business-Angel-Reportweb.pdf

33   https://www.british-business-bank.co.uk/wp-content/uploads/2018/06/Business-Angel-Reportweb.pdf

34   https://www.washingtonpost.com/sf/brand-connect/allstate/fewer-millennials-are-buying-real-estate-is-that-a-bad-thing

35   https://www.washingtonpost.com/sf/brand-connect/allstate/fewer-millennials-are-buying-real-estate-is-that-a-bad-thing/

36   https://www.cnbc.com/2021/04/01/housing-costs-prove-challenging-for-many-older-millennials.html

37   https://www.un.org/africarenewal/magazine/special-edition-women-2012/women-struggle-secure-land-rights

38   https://www.glamourmagazine.co.uk/article/gender-mortgage-gap

39   https://www.weforum.org/agenda/2017/01/women-own-less-than-20-of-the-worlds-land-its-time-to-give-them-equal-property-rights/

40   https://rentalhousingjournal.com/more-than-50-percent-of-millenials-now-own-homes/

41   https://www.propertyinvestortoday.co.uk/breaking-news/2021/7/investors--women-total-48-of-uks-buy-to-let-investors

42   https://nlihc.org/resource/study-finds-housing-market-discrimination-contributes-racial-disparities-exposure

43   https://www.impactinvest.org.uk/events/report-launch-is-there-an-investment-case-for-social-and-affordable-housing-in-the-uk/

44   https://www.ftadviser.com/ftadviser-focus/2021/09/08/how-to-understand-trends-in-women-s-home-ownership/

Chapter 7

1   https://www.ifc.org/wps/wcm/connect/topics_ext_content/ifc_external_corporate_site/development+impact/principles

2   https://www.spglobal.com/marketintelligence/en/news-insights/latest-news-headlines/esg-funds-beat-out-s-p-500-in-1st-year-of-covid-19-how-1-fund-shot-to-the-top-63224550

3   https://www.mckinsey.com/~/media/McKinsey/Business%20Functions/Strategy%20and%20Corporate%20Finance/Our%20Insights/Five%20ways%20that%20ESG%20creates%20value/Five-ways-that-ESG-creates-value.ashx

4   https://www.fool.com/retirement/strategies/asset-allocation-by-age/

5   https://www.theguardian.com/us-news/2019/may/25/american-pain-society-doctors-painkillers

6   https://labs.theguardian.com/unicef-child-labour/

Chapter 8

1   Lee, Young-joo. (2014). The feminine sector: Explaining the overrepresentation of women in the nonprofit sector in the USA. International Journal of Social Economics. 41. 556-572. 10.1108/IJSE-01-2013-0011
2   https://80000hours.org/key-ideas/
3   https://www.idea.int/sites/default/files/publications/political-finance-regulations-around-the-world.pdf
4   https://www.idea.int/sites/default/files/publications/political-finance-regulations-around-the-world.pdf
5   https://www.downtoearth.org.in/coverage/chipko-an-unfinished-mission-30883
6   *Principles of Microeconomics.* https://openstax.org/details/books/principles-microeconomics. Adapted from Figure 6.7 - "A Backward-Bending Supply Curve of Labor".
7   https://thehappinessindex.com/blog/can-money-make-you-happy
8   https://www.wsj.com/articles/even-for-the-very-rich-more-money-brings-happiness-1512662638

Chapter 9

1   Astghik Mavisakalyan, Yashar Tarverdi, Gender and climate change: Do female parliamentarians make difference?, European Journal of Political Economy, Volume 56, 2019, Pages 151-164, ISSN 0176-2680, https://doi.org/10.1016j.ejpoleco.2018.08.001 (https://www.sciencedirect.com/science/article/pii/S0176268017304500); https://yaleclimateconnections.org/2019/09/countries-with-more-female-politicians-pass-more-ambitious-climate-policies-study-suggests/
2   https://www.kcl.ac.uk/news/women-political-leaders-key-to-more-equal-and-caring-societies
3   https://www.un.org/en/desa/we-must-achieve-it-now-current-a nd-future-generations
4   https://www.fraserinstitute.org/sites/default/files/is-climate-catastrophe-really-10-years-away.pdf

Index

About the Authors

This book is about changing the world with money, and we've dedicated our lives to doing just that. How? By starting our company Female Invest, educating women in 100+ countries on how to manage their money and begin investing.

Female Invest started out as a passion project when we met in Business School, and the original idea was to find a group of 10-20 women who could support each other on their investment journeys. However, things didn't go as planned. Thousands of women found us on social media, and we ended up hosting in-person events for 25,000 women alongside our studies.

The verdict was clear: our own search for female investors was a symptom of a much bigger problem. Today, women are falling financially behind in every country in the world. This is highly problematic, because money equals power, freedom, and independence. Realizing that changed everything, our lives soon revolved around the mission of closing the financial gender gap. After a year and a half, we took the leap to become full-time entrepreneurs. We had no money, no network, and no experience. Taking the leap is the scariest and hardest thing we've ever done, and, without comparison, the most meaningful and exciting thing we've ever done.

To date, 400,000+ women have taken our courses. We've raised $12 million, breaking glass ceilings in a world where women (sadly) raise just 2% of funding. We're proud to be recognized by Forbes on their "30 Under 30" list and by trailblazing women such as Emma Watson and Hillary Clinton, who both got the first book *Girls Just Wanna Have Funds. A Feminist Guide to Investing.*

A lot has happened, but the journey has only just begun. Because we won't stop until women have the same financial possibilities as men. We invite anyone who supports this mission to join the movement and own their financial future in the name of a new status quo.

Are you ready?

We are especially grateful to the experts who have sparred with us along the way to make this book as good as possible. A special thanks to Cecilie Simiab, Senior Specialist in ESG & Carbon Business Development at Nasdaq; Torsten Bech, Senior Analyst and Senior Portfolio Manager at Maj Invest; Mads Willumsen, Co-founder of sustainable investment platform Gaia Investments; and Zoe Burt, Certified Financial Advisor.

DK UK

Editorial Director Cara Armstrong
Project Editor Izzy Holton
US Executive Editor Lori Hand
Senior Designer Tania Gomes
Managing Editor Ruth O'Rourke
Senior Production Editor Tony Phipps
Senior Production Controller
Luca Bazzoli
Jacket and Sales Material
Coordinator Emily Cannings
Art Director Max Pedliham
Publishing Director Katie Cowan

Editorial Helena Caldon
Design Bess Daly
Americanization Jen Wilson-Farley

First American Edition, 2023
Published in the United States
by DK Publishing
1450 Broadway, 20th Floor,
New York, NY 10019

Copyright © 2023
Dorling Kindersley Limited
DK, a Division of
Penguin Random House LLC
23 24 25 26 27 28 10 9 8 7 6 5 4 3 2 1
001–334484–Nov/2023

Published in Great Britain by Dorling
Kindersley Limited.

A catalog record for this book
is available from the
Library of Congress.

ISBN: 978-0-7440-8545-7

Printed and bound in Slovakia

www.dk.com